EVERYONE CAN BE A
★ NINJA ★

EVERYONE CAN BE A ★NINJA★

FIND YOUR INNER WARRIOR
AND ACHIEVE YOUR DREAMS

AKBAR GBAJABIAMILA

GALLERY BOOKS

New York London Toronto Sydney New Delhi

G

Gallery Books
An Imprint of Simon & Schuster, Inc.
1230 Avenue of the Americas
New York, NY 10020

First Gallery Books hardcover edition May 2019

GALLERY BOOKS and colophon are registered trademarks of Simon & Schuster, Inc.

For information about special discounts for bulk purchases, please contact Simon & Schuster Special Sales at 1-866-506-1949 or business@simonandschuster.com.

The Simon & Schuster Speakers Bureau can bring authors to your live event. For more information or to book an event, contact the Simon & Schuster Speakers Bureau at 1-866-248-3049 or visit our website at www.simonspeakers.com.

Interior design by Jaime Putorti

Manufactured in the United States of America

10   9   8   7   6   5   4   3   2   1

Library of Congress Cataloging-in-Publication Data is available.

ISBN 978-1-9821-0975-2
ISBN 978-1-9821-0977-6 (ebook)

Raising four kids is truly a blessing from God to my wife and me, and it comes with a tremendous responsibility. When you're in the trenches of parenting, you can get caught up in directing instead of connecting. So I want to dedicate this book to my children, Elijah, Saheedat, Nasir, and Naomi, whom I love dearly. You know me affectionately as Dad, but I hope that this book will give you insight into my life experiences and a little more context to who I am as a person.

CONTENTS

TIME TO BEGIN

April 10, 2013, was probably the worst day I ever had in my career. It was also my first day on the set of *American Ninja Warrior*. When I arrived at the Venice Beach location that afternoon, I was trembling with excitement and nerves. The enormity of the moment and what the opportunity meant for me was in the forefront of my mind. *Don't blow this*, I told myself. I was scared, but it was a good fear, a respectful fear. The job was bigger than any I had had in my four years of broadcasting. As a former NFL athlete, I had gotten my start calling college football games, offering insightful analysis and color commentary to augment the action on the field. It was a medium I had worked hard to master up to this point, and I believed that the effort I had put into my craft would show on *ANW*.

What I quickly learned when I entered broadcasting is that to talk well in front of a camera isn't natural; it's a skill I had to learn. The way you talk to your friends and family just doesn't work when you're talking to millions of viewers. I spent years developing this new skill and I became good at it—good enough at least to land a spot on the NFL Network, and then on *ANW*. I knew the format would be slightly different, but the gist was the same: The audience would *feel* my words; they would be able to *taste* my excitement, as each competitor jumped, climbed, and pulled their way to the next obstacle. At the same time, I understood the stage I was entering was larger than any I had ever walked on. The show was in its fifth season and had a passionate, devoted fan base. Would they accept the new guy whose claim to fame was football? Would I be able to understand this compelling, new sport well enough to analyze, dissect, and appreciate what these amazing ninjas were doing?

I felt like I could. I had spent the previous month since being hired watching countless episodes as a crash course on all things *Ninja Warrior*. I felt ready. This was my moment. There I sat in my trailer, about to go out and tape the introduction.

Someone hands me a script. "Memorize this!" I look down and see more than a hundred words staring back at me on the page. I look at the clock. Thirty minutes till taping. Thirty minutes to memorize this? It's possible, if everyone could get out of my trailer and give me time to concentrate. But that's not how television works. You're never alone on set. I hold the script to my face as someone applies the makeup. I look at the clock. Twenty-five minutes. Someone else enters my trailer.

"New script!" they cry, handing me another sheet of paper.

New script? What about the one I had spent five minutes absorbing? Never mind that. Please, would everyone just leave me alone for the next twenty minutes? I stare at the script, digesting the words. A sudden fear grips me: This isn't my voice. I don't talk like this. . . .

Wardrobe! Have you ever tried to memorize something while someone helps you dress? Because I never had. I look at the clock. Fifteen minutes.

My stomach grumbles, and I suddenly remember that I'm going to be on set for four hours without a break. I look around for some food, reading the script as I cram something in my mouth. Then I think about the bathroom. I should probably go. Four hours is a long time.

I look at the clock. Ten minutes. No time. *Keep reading. Keep memorizing.* Do I have it? I try to recite the script and stumble on the first sentence. I don't have it. I look at the clock. Five minutes. Time is running out.

Then I'm rushed out of my trailer and hurried to the spot in front of the cameras. My cohost, Matt Iseman, a veteran of the show since Season 2, is already there, looking cool and collected. Someone pushes me onto my mark; the lights are blinding. Someone else shoves an earpiece in my ear, and voices come alive in my head. More talking, more directing, someone screaming, "Smile!" I break out into a smile, maybe because it's the only thing I can understand at that moment. Someone else yells, "Action," and I'm on. It's on. It's starting. My moment. My chance. My opportunity. Here we go!

And I bomb.

The jumble of words in my head makes no sense. I try to repeat them, I try to remember, but they don't come out. They stop the cameras. I try to collect myself. We go again. "Action!" But I can't do it. I stumble over the words. It's a cool night on Venice Beach, but I'm in a cold sweat. I can feel the heat of humiliation in my stomach, the streams of perspiration dripping down my forehead. Suddenly, I panic. I can't remember what I just said.

I go several more times, and still nothing. Then I get a bright idea. "Can we use a teleprompter?" I ask. I had never used a teleprompter before, but how hard could it be?

Someone rolls out a teleprompter. Great! This will work . . . except I can't read a teleprompter. It sounds so stupid—and you feel so stupid when you can't do it. I feel like everyone looking at me is thinking the same thing: *Can't this guy read?* This went straight to the heart of my insecurities as a child and a student— that little kid inside me who always suspected I wasn't smart enough. Except that I could read. I loved to read. So why couldn't I read a teleprompter? I don't know, but what made it all worse was that I was the one who had suggested it!

Eventually, the executive producer decides to end my suffering. "Why don't we just go to the runs?" they say, meaning, let's go to the live-action part of the taping. It was the part of the job at which I felt most confident, because it required those skills I had honed calling live football games. There aren't any "takes" or scripts to memorize. The competitors take their turns in quick succession and Matt and I do our thing. But I'm already in my own head. My focus is shot. My confidence is in tatters. My career? My career is likely finished.

How did I ever think I was good enough to do this?

My whole life I have had to fight to achieve my dreams. Since I was a child growing up in South Central Los Angeles to that first day on the set to today, I have faced moments of trial, hardship, and extreme, almost crippling, self-doubt. Yet we live in an age that doesn't have much patience for feelings of inadequacy. Sure, we're told we can fail, time and again. The great ones of sports, business, tech, politics, and the arts have all failed. Failure is part of success! We get that. I get that. And, boy, have I failed spectacularly. But to admit that we can't do something? That we aren't good enough? We recoil at the thought. Admitting weakness lets people behind the curtain of our carefully constructed image—an image we nurture on social media, on holiday cards, and even within our own circle of friends—of a happy, confident, successful person. Look at my beautiful family! Look at my beautiful career! Look at my beautiful life! Don't you wish you had the things I do?

But failure, hardship, obstacles—these aren't the things that hold us back. What holds us back is the little voice that whispers: "You're not good enough." This voice comes to us when we dare to imagine ourselves achieving something truly great. It's a voice that is quiet, but sinister. It can destroy our confidence before we ever set foot on the course. Before we've had a chance to see if we can overcome that obstacle staring us in the face, the voice tells us we can't—so why try? It's so much easier and safer to present an image of success than to walk the hard road of confronting our own insecurities.

Yet as I reflect on my own life, I see those moments when the voice nearly overcame my desire to succeed, and I wonder where I would be had I listened to it. I wouldn't be the host of *American Ninja Warrior*. I wouldn't be on the NFL Network. I wouldn't have made the NFL as an undrafted free agent. I wouldn't have made it out of my neighborhood of South Central Los Angeles. I wouldn't be who I am. I wouldn't be what God wanted me to be. That first day on the set of *ANW* wasn't the worst for me because it was hard. It was the worst because it seemed to confirm that voice in my head, the one that said I wasn't good enough. I didn't belong there. I shouldn't have aimed so high.

Because we're unwilling to admit to one another that this voice exists, we too often think that we're alone. That *we're* the only ones who feel this way. Everyone else seems to pursue their dreams and ambitions just fine! What's wrong with us? What's wrong with me?

That was the seed for this book. I realized that I wasn't alone. Everyone has these fears and moments of agonizing self-doubt. Some of us can overcome them; many of us can't. What separates the ones who do from the ones who don't? What separates me, someone who has found some success, from someone who can't seem to put it all together? I have been blessed many times in my life with people who have helped me overcome not just my own doubts but the obstacles and hardships that blocked my own journey. They helped me see the solutions, the answers to the riddles that boggled me. Some were mentors, some were friends, some have been ninjas on the show, and two were my parents.

The lessons I have learned from them all have helped me achieve the things I wanted in life. But I'm still learning. I would never say that I have "made it." I don't look at my dreams this way. I am on a journey that never ends, and I want you to walk with me down this road. This book is a collection of the lessons and ideas that I have learned over my life so far. In looking back on what I have done, and trying to understand how I did it, I see patterns and themes. Over and over, I see something that resembles a game plan. Now, I can't say that I consciously followed this game plan my whole life, but I did accomplish the goals I had set for myself, whether as a child growing up with dreams of an athletic career or pursuing my passion for broadcasting. I know what it takes to get me to the point on the horizon that God has told me to go to.

And if I have learned these things, then I want you to know them as well. I don't believe that success is something that is reserved for a select few who have the right amount of determination, work ethic, and discipline. What separates those who have achieved their dreams and goals in life from those who haven't isn't luck. It isn't that they're better. I'm not better than anyone. I was blessed with talents that God wanted me to hone and strengthen *so that* I could do what He wanted me to do. But everyone is blessed with talents and strengths, and our dreams—those wistful ideas that seem so unrealistic, yet draw us out of our safe, comfortable lives—are messages from God. This is where He wants us to go.

But the journey isn't meant to be easy. Obstacles will confront us from the very beginning. Before we even lace up our shoes, we'll encounter them. We might even find the strength and determination to overcome the first one, and then the next one. Then we will find an obstacle in our path that we don't think we can overcome. And that's what stops us. It's not that we have a problem getting started; it's that we have a problem with consistency.

Success isn't always about being the best. It's about applying ourselves consistently so that we train our minds and bodies to confront each fresh obstacle as we confronted the previous ones: with determination, fortitude, and confidence. Consistent hard work will lead to success. And continual success leads to greatness.

Despite my first day—despite my first season—I have spent the past six years as cohost of *American Ninja Warrior*. I love my job. Every season, I am blessed to witness hundreds of men and women realize their dreams of competing on the show. Most of the competitors aren't—and have never been—professional athletes. Their stories of how they made it to that starting line represent only part of what has made the show so popular. The other half is then watching them overcome obstacles so demanding that most won't even make it to the final challenge, the 14.5-foot Warped Wall, atop of which is a buzzer you must press to officially complete the course. And if you are one of the millions of viewers tuning in each week, then you know how excited I can get for these competitors. I scream, I wince, I laugh, I cry, and I root enthusiastically for each one of them. Yet the show, while a competition, is unique in one important aspect: Most of the ninjas who step up to the starting line know they won't get through the course. It's a dynamic that I believe is special to the show; in fact, I think it's one of the reasons the show has grown in such popularity over the years. Most of the competitors aren't there to win. They're there because they fought for their chance to be there. They are everyday Americans: single mothers, cancer survivors, former athletes, nonathletes, nine-to-fivers, and those who are unemployed. Some are young, some are old, some have diseases, while others struggle with a disability or an addiction. They are underdogs. They aren't supposed to be there.

But none of that matters. Because at that moment, by stepping up on that platform, with the cameras rolling and the crowd cheering, they have already won. They have become great, even if they aren't the greatest. They have overcome whatever circumstances might hold them back, whatever weakness has plagued their lives, and whatever doubt and fear told them they couldn't do it. And yet they have proved beyond any doubt that they belong on that course. They are good enough.

How did they get there? Why are they there? Why didn't they just stay home? Why did they bother to endure all the pain, all the sweat, all the sacrifice to attempt something they know they'll likely fail at?

I realized that the answers to these questions could be found in my own journey toward achieving my dreams. Too many of us believe that if we can't be the greatest, then we shouldn't try. Yet never in my career have I been the greatest at anything. Not when I was in the NFL, and certainly not now. But was my goal to play in the NFL any less realized because I will never have a bronze bust in the Hall of Fame? No, because I accomplished what I had set out to do—a dream that was first formed while a teenager growing up in the rough neighborhoods of Crenshaw, Los Angeles; nurtured while I played in college on a scholarship, even as I experienced the tragedy of my mother's passing; and finally realized the moment the Raiders took a chance on an undrafted free agent. Not once during my NFL career did I feel secure in my position. I fought tooth and nail to make it to another season, to play well enough to make it onto the field. If this book was about how to be the greatest, then I wouldn't be the one to write it.

Rather, this book is how everyone can achieve their dreams. And by doing *that*, we become great.

A brief word on the title: Many times over my tenure as host of *American Ninja Warrior*, I have spoken with fans of the show who have said to me, "You know, I think I could do what those ninjas do."

So why don't they? If they think they can do it, then why aren't they doing it?

More to the point: Why aren't you pursuing your dreams right now?

My answer is that many people simply don't know how. They don't know where to start, what to do, and where to go. They can't decide what to give up or what to focus on. They don't know who to ask for help or if they should ask for help at all. And, finally, they don't think they can.

You can. *Everyone* can. That is why I titled this book *Everyone Can Be a Ninja*, because God has blessed all of us with talents and gifts and He has given us a vision for how to use them. Our dreams are His vision for us. We are *supposed* to strive for them. We are *supposed* to find greatness. We are *meant* to be ninjas in whatever way we define that word.

I started this book with an example of failure from my own life because I want you to see in my struggles your own struggles. I want you to see that you can relate to a six-feet-six former NFL athlete with an unusual name. As such, I rely on the triumphs and failures of my own life to impart the lessons I have learned.

I grew up in South Central Los Angeles with dreams of becoming a basketball player, but found my calling in football instead. I earned a scholarship to San Diego State University, where my older brother Kabeer also played football, and performed well enough to expect to get drafted into the NFL. Only that didn't happen for me. I went undrafted but found a spot on the Oakland Raiders as a free agent. Making the NFL was the realization of a dream, a completion of a goal I had set for myself. I was a good football player, but never great. Every season I played I was in danger of getting cut. In fact I was cut, a couple of times, and bounced around the league, looking for that next team to give me a chance. During my NFL career, I also started to pursue broadcasting. I knew it was an industry I wanted to go into after my playing days were over, but I also knew that I wouldn't be able to rely on my superstardom to get a job. If someone was going to hire me to be on television, it would be because I was a good broadcaster who fully understood the game, not for my football credentials. So I did radio and television analysis while still a player just to get a feel for the game. After I retired, I threw myself into broadcasting with everything I had. I was fortunate to get a job with the now-defunct Mtn. Network and then CBS College Sports Network, calling college games, but it was a struggle, financially and personally. My first big break came when I was hired by the NFL Network to join *Fantasy Live*. Less than a year later, I was the cohost of *American Ninja Warrior*, where I remain to this day.

That's my career biography, and it has been a successful career. But biographies tell only part of the story. This book tells you the other, more interesting part of the story: the stuff that happens in between. No one who is successful got there by chance. Success, the realization of dreams, doesn't just happen. I worked hard to get to where I am today, but hard work isn't the only thing one needs to be successful. As I look back over my career, I see patterns, behaviors, and skills that helped me. Often I didn't realize what I was doing or how I did it until years later, but this book is the summation of what I have learned and what I believe allowed me to achieve my dreams. As such, each chapter in this book is devoted to a specific lesson or idea that I believe helped me get to where I am today. I have tried to follow a chronological telling of my life, yet jumps from one stage of my life to the next are unavoidable. I want you to pay more attention to the ideas and themes being discussed.

But I never wanted this book to be just about me. No one realizes their dreams on their own, and I am so grateful to those men and women whose examples of sacrifice, heroism, and sheer grit have made me who I am today. As such, each chapter will also feature the story of someone from my life who I believe supports, augments, or, in some cases, presents a different take on the ideas and lessons being discussed. You'll find people who have inspired me, helped me, and taught me so much, including some of the *ANW* competitors I rooted for from my cohosting perch above the courses. I must give thanks to the producers of the show, who were the ones who found these inspiring and amazing ninjas in the first place. Fans of the show will recognize many. For those who have never heard of Jimmy Choi, Kacy Catanzaro, or Zach Gowen, you are in for a treat. It was difficult to whittle down the list to those who appear in the book, but, as I think you'll agree, their stories are truly amazing.

At its core, this book presents a simple idea: that our journeys toward our dreams aren't all that different. Whether your dream is to compete on a television show, to run a marathon, to start a company, to overcome a personal condition, or simply to live a better, more fulfilling life, we all must pass through a similar gauntlet. We all experience similar tests, doubts, fears, sacrifices, and failures. We all must learn how to overcome them. We are all different, and we all want different things from life, but I believe the connective threads that bind us reveal that we can find a path forward together. My hope is that by the end of the book, you will not only feel inspired to start your own journey; you'll know how to start and how to keep going. You won't just have a little boost to get out of bed one morning; you will *know* how to get out of bed every morning and make a difference in your life. Inspiring stories and motivational words aren't enough to find your inner ninja. You need to act. You need a game plan. You need to know how to begin.

1

MAKE THEM SAY YOUR NAME

The first time I played football I hated it. I was a junior in high school and I was—and had always wanted to be—a basketball player. I was good at basketball, but I wasn't great. By my junior year I had progressed from where I had started as a freshman, and my chances of making the varsity squad had improved. This is no small thing at Crenshaw High School, which has one of the best basketball programs in the country. It was my dream to make that varsity team. I had spent nearly my entire childhood honing my basketball skills, trying to overcome a talent deficit that I refused to admit existed.

At the same time I was struggling with basketball, my brother Kabeer was a football star at Crenshaw High School. My brother is two years older than me and had the same commitment to football that I had to basketball. He was highly focused and precise about the way he played the game. But he had a quality that I didn't have: an innate skill for his chosen game. Kabeer was widely recruited by colleges and in his senior year was named the Los Angeles Defensive Lineman of the Year.

My brother and I were somewhat similar in size. But to those who didn't know us, and who would judge us on our physical presence alone, I would have seemed to be the better athlete: I was slightly taller and had more weight on me. (A defensive end, Kabeer was tall, fast, and extremely strong, but he always struggled to keep his weight on.) I may have looked more like a football player than my brother did, but today, Kabeer is in the Green Bay Packers Hall of Fame. This goes to show how useful appearances are. I'm not going to be in anyone's hall of fame (for sports, at least), but at that time in our lives, outsiders—specifically, hungry varsity football coaches—would think that I might become a better player.

As I entered my junior year at Crenshaw, Kabeer went off to play Division I ball at San Diego State University. Meanwhile, Crenshaw's head football coach, Robert Garrett, had been after me for years to try football. I had absolutely no interest in the game, but I had seen my brother's success get him a ride to a Division I school. If he could do it, couldn't I? I decided to give it a try.

The challenge, of course, was that I didn't have any experience, knowledge, or passion for the game. I showed up to my first practice in basketball shoes because I didn't have cleats. That didn't stop the coaches from finding some old size 15 Adidas cleats and shoving them on my feet. I looked at the pads they had given me and had no idea what went where. I ended up putting my shoulder pads on backward, my thigh pads inside out, and my knee pads upside down. I was a mess. Then they stuck a helmet on my head and sent me out to tackle some guys.

I hated it. Everything I loved about basketball—the grace of dribbling, the angling for position, the symmetry of the perfect shot and rebound—all of that was gone. In its place was this barbaric sport of smashing my body against someone else's. *Find the ball! Where's the ball? Go to the ball! How can I find the ball when I can't see a foot in front of my face? How can I tackle anyone when two guys are pushing against me with all their weight?*

I am not a crier, but I will admit that I cried beneath my helmet on that first day of practice. I had spent years trying to improve my basketball game to the point where I belonged on the court. Now out on the field, I was again that lanky, uncoordinated kid who didn't deserve to be part of the team. The coaches had expected me to play as well as my brother, and I felt that I was disappointing them. I wanted to go back to the sport I knew and I loved.

So I quit.

A CHILD IN THE HOOD

I am a first-generation American from a big, complicated family. Growing up, there were nine of us: two parents, six boys, and a girl. I was child number six, sandwiched between twins (a boy and the girl) and a younger brother not too far behind.

My parents came to the United States in the early 1970s from Nigeria and settled in the Los Angeles area. My father, Mustapha, had the entrepreneurial spirit that defines a lot of immigrants who come to America looking for opportunity. After a series of jobs, he started work as a plumbing technician for Melvin's Rooter. Several years later, he had saved enough money to set up his own plumbing business. He worked out of an old blue Chevrolet van emblazoned with the company name, "Express Rooter," and our home phone number, always letting people know that he offered "twenty-four-hour service." He was a great plumber; he took calls around the clock every day of the week, went out on every call he received, devoted whatever time was necessary to fix his clients' plumbing problems, and charged a fair wage for his services. Before the days of Yelp or Angie's List, small-business owners like my father relied on word-of-mouth advertising, and the word about him was excellent. People respected his work and they respected him.

My mother had her own business as well. She did hair, and her clients loved her. "Lady B," they called her, short for her first name, Bolatito. Like my father, she was there for her clients whenever they needed her regardless of the day and regardless of the hour. (I learned that hair emergencies are real.) My parents modeled for us an incredibly strong work ethic that they, in turn, expected us to bring to everything we did, whether it was academics, sports, or chores.

But beyond sharing a mutual homeland, work ethic, and commitment to raising their children, my parents had almost nothing in common. My father consistently carried himself with a quiet strength, while my mother could be loud, dramatic, and emotionally complex. My mother's erratic behavior had a simple explanation—simple, but no less tragic and painful for her and for her family. She was an alcoholic. Her drinking led to wild swings in behavior and often resulted in terrible confrontations inside our home. Our house should have been a place of safety for us, a fortress protecting us from the dangers and temptations outside our front door. But my mother's drinking often made life at home just as chaotic and frightening as anything the hood offered. My father and mother fought constantly, often in their native tongue of Yoruba. My siblings and I did not know precisely what they were saying, but we deeply felt the cruelty of their words and it was horrible. I would escape from these charged moments at home to the basketball court down the street.

Looking back, I realize now that it must have been a tremendous struggle for my parents to raise seven children on the pay of a plumber and a hairdresser. Our house was big and beautiful in my eyes, but the reality was that it was in the middle of a neighborhood that at the time was one of the toughest in Los Angeles.

We lived in the Crenshaw District in South Central Los Angeles. When I was growing up, South Central was rightly considered one of the most dangerous areas in the country. Today, the community has done a lot to turn itself around, but at that time, South Central was best known for its gangs, drugs, and drive-by shootings. Still, the list of notable alumni from Crenshaw High is impressive and includes sports figures like Darryl Strawberry, Olympians like Johnny Gray Jr., politicians like James Butts, and rappers like Ice-T. *Boyz n the Hood*, which came out when I was in elementary school, was set in my neighborhood and at my high school. The film, directed by John Singleton, was in many ways autobiographical for me. The story of how Ricky, Tre's friend, tried to avoid the violence and gang life around him to focus on his football dreams resonated with me. The film was a critical and commercial success, but beyond the accolades, it gave voice to many of the challenges of growing up in my community.

To an outsider, it might be difficult to imagine how all seven of us stayed out of trouble, but my parents were strong-willed and strict. They had come to America to build a better life and were determined that their children would succeed. My father was a patriarch in every sense; he ruled the family and his word was law. One didn't disobey Dad. In our household, any infraction or form of disrespect would result in strict punishment.

My parents were painfully aware of the dangers beyond the doors of our home. My father tried to ensure our safety by exerting total control over our environment. Just down the street from our corner-lot house there was a low stone-brick wall that lined the property of one of our neighbors' houses. It wasn't more than a hundred feet from our front yard, but it marked the limit on how far we could ride our bikes. My father wouldn't allow us to go beyond the stone wall. I've never forgotten that, because it forced me to see two things: first, that there were dangers in the world beyond our control, and second, that my father's rules had a purpose, as much as we kids chafed at them. My parents realized that beyond the physical dangers, our neighborhood offered temptations that could steer us off their chosen path for us. They embraced American culture but they also brought with them ideas from Nigeria, the foremost of which was the primacy of education. Everything we did as kids took second place to education. I can't speak for the parents of my friends, but by and large in our neighborhood athletics was seen as the only way out. We understood our parents' devotion to education, but for us, we studied because that's what we had to do. Our father ruled our home with an iron fist, and we studied to avoid his wrath. We were a tight-knit family that loved to have fun and joke around, but we spoke to our parents and to one another with respect. We never swore. We were expected to get good grades. We were expected to be honest and to keep our word.

We were also expected to pray. Although my parents were both extremely religious, they followed different paths to God. My father practiced Islam, while my mother was a Christian. In our household, prayer was not a choice. It was required. Each morning, my siblings and I gathered to say our Muslim prayers in Arabic and our Christian prayers in English. I didn't have a clear idea of exactly what I was saying, but that early exposure to prayer had a profound effect on me. I learned to believe in something more powerful than myself. As a child, it didn't matter to me if He was from the Muslim faith or the Christian. What mattered was that I learned devotion to Him. There would come a time when this devotion needed more substance, and questions needed to be answered. But I am deeply grateful to my parents for instilling in me a belief in God, without whom I wouldn't be who or what I am today.

Like most kids, I wanted desperately to fit in, but as is often the situation with immigrant children, many factors conspired to make me different. The kids I went to school with shared my skin color, but we had little else in common. All my siblings experienced the same ridicule. The kids teased us relentlessly about our African heritage. They sported Air Jordans and hip-hop-inspired street wear, while my parents occasionally had us attend school in traditional Nigerian dress. We stood out (and not in a good way) in dashikis and knockoff Jordans.

More than anything, though, the kids laughed at me for my name. To them, it was a string of incompatible letters thrown together for their amusement. They took joy in butchering my last name and taunting me for my first. (Thank goodness they didn't know about my middle name!)

My teachers weren't much better, although in fairness they were not trying to make fun of me. As a means of self-preservation, I learned to shout, "That's me! That's me!" during roll call seconds before my teachers had a chance to mispronounce my last name.

There were times I wanted to curse my last name, and my first name wasn't much better. I had never met another Akbar in my life and nobody could pronounce—let alone spell—Gbajabiamila. (It looks a lot scarier than it is. Don't say the "G" and pronounce the rest, and you have it.) Rather than feeling unique or special, I felt lonely and strange.

My dad was sympathetic to the way his last name intimidated non-Nigerians. When he came to the U.S., he even spelled it Gbaja-biamila, adding the hyphen for a time, to make it easier for Americans to say. But he did not understand or sympathize with my feelings about avoiding my name completely. He told me I should feel the confidence, strength, and power that my name conveyed. In the African culture, the naming of a child is extremely important, and I had been named deliberately: *Akbar Oluwakemi-Idowu Gbajabiamila*.

I had been taught how to correctly pronounce (and spell!) my entire name at an early age. More important, I had been carefully schooled in the meaning of each word. *Akbar* is Arabic for "great." *Oluwakemi* means "God blessed me" in my parents' native tongue of Yoruba, and *Idowu*, also Yoruba, means "born after twins" (referring to my older twin siblings—my brother, Kabeer, and my sister, Kubrat). *Gbajabiamila* means "big man, come save me."

"Make them say your name!" my dad would urge me in his thick Nigerian accent, when my teachers butchered my name or my friends tried to make fun of it. "It is your name! Make them say it! Make them say your name!"

As a child, I wanted nothing more than to have a name like all the other kids. I wanted to dress like all the other kids and go by a "normal" name like Jason Smith or Dexter Gordon. My heroes at the time—including Earvin "Magic" Johnson and Michael Jordan—all had "normal" names. Why couldn't I?

Today, however, I am so grateful for my name, which was carefully chosen by my father, and each day I endeavor to live up to it:

★ *Akbar*—I strive to be great.
★ *Oluwakemi*—I am grateful for the blessings of God.
★ *Idowu*—My commitment is to family.
★ *Gbajabiamila*—I live my life in service to others.

By the seventh grade, I had had enough. I was sick of the teasing and the bias against Africans. I realized that my only option, other than to embrace the temptations of the hood and find my identity in the gang culture, was to embrace who I was. I forced myself to take pride in my African heritage, going so far as to say that I was Nigerian, not American. Today, I am both, but when I was an adolescent my identity pendulum had swung so completely toward the African side of me that I could finally walk proudly, and start my life as Akbar.

FINDING MY PLACE

The story of my childhood is a story of fears, doubts, and insecurities. But it's also a story of overcoming them. I ran up against seemingly insurmountable obstacles that blocked my path. I felt the urge to throw in the towel, call it quits, and slide into a life that was just a little bit easier, a little bit safer, and a whole lot less frightening.

Entering my freshman year of high school, I was fifteen years

old and at six feet, two inches tall, I had little control over my lanky body. But through my older brother Willie, I had discovered the joy of basketball. I committed fully to the game, vowing to improve my skills no matter the cost. It was, after all, where kids "like me" made a name for themselves. We knew the odds of playing in the NBA were steep, but for many of us it felt like the only way to escape a life in the inner city.

I could not have picked a more competitive sport. Crenshaw High School had built a dynasty where basketball was concerned. Every year, more than three hundred kids tried out for the team. Only a handful made it. Coach Willie West Jr. was considered one of the best high school basketball coaches of all time. In his thirty-seven years coaching at Crenshaw, he led his teams to more than eight hundred victories. His teams won a record eight state titles, sixteen Los Angeles City Section titles, and twenty-eight league titles. His 1985 team finished the season 31–0, traveled to Denmark, and won the High School International Tournament Championship.

Coach West coached several players who made it to the NBA, including Marques Johnson. More than forty of his players went on to play at four-year colleges, including former Cal State LA men's basketball coach and current Oregon State assistant coach Stephen Thompson, who starred at Syracuse. In 1995 the Crenshaw High School basketball gym was renamed the Willie E. West Jr. Pavilion. I played under Coach West for two years at Crenshaw High. I played on the junior varsity team before moving to varsity in my junior year. During that year and the next, our team won

back-to-back city and state championships. It felt good to be a winner.

With the rich history of basketball at Crenshaw, maybe now my decision to quit football makes more sense. My whole life was basketball. I believed with all my heart that I would one day make the pros (which was about as likely as my becoming a professional tennis player). I gave football a try because I saw my brother's success and assumed I could play as well, despite never having stepped onto a football field. After a week, I had decided I hated it. That's why I quit.

My father, however, would have none of it. He marched me right back to the football field. "If you start it, you will finish it," he proclaimed.

Frankly, I was surprised at my father's reaction. Here in America, many parents are deeply involved in their children's sports activities, but to my Nigerian father, athletics were a distraction. Even though he and my mother loved much about American culture, they held on to many of the biases and assumptions from their homeland. One of these was that high school sports were not a serious pursuit; they were a pastime. My parents did not travel thousands upon thousands of miles so their kids could become athletes. They wanted us to become doctors or lawyers or business professionals. They wanted us to hold "real" jobs that required a real education.

Which is why they almost never came to my games. In fact, I don't believe my mother came to one of my basketball or football games in junior high or high school. I had to beg my father to come to a game of mine, and he managed to make a couple. I can

still recall, before leaving the house for school, yelling up the stairs to my parents to remind them I had a game that night. It didn't make much difference.

And when you're a child, your parents' interest in your activities is the whole world. I thought that they didn't want to watch me play because I wasn't good enough, but I now know that it had nothing to do with me—my parents didn't go to any of their kids' games. They put a greater priority on work and providing for the family.

So why did my father care whether I played football?

To my father, quitting the football team wasn't about football. It was about not fulfilling a commitment, and that was not acceptable behavior for a Gbajabiamila. We had been raised to believe that our word was our promise. I had told the coaches I would play football, and I would complete what I started. My father informed me that I would play the entire season of football—whether I wanted to or not. He told me he would not allow me to walk away from something simply because I wasn't good at it. If we only did the things we were good at, he said, then we wouldn't achieve anything.

So, for an entire season, I endured feelings of inadequacy. Every day, I operated so far outside my comfort zone that I cried. Every day, I confronted this lanky kid in the mirror who didn't understand how to read the playbook or didn't have the skills his brother had to make the tackle. (I didn't consider, of course, that my brother had played football since elementary school. I was only in my first year.)

My coach, Coach Garrett, did not let me forget that day that I quit the team. In fact, I didn't even get to play in a real game until the last two games of the season, when Coach put me in for a few snaps. He worked me hard and made me earn my place. Eventually, even with the limited exposure, the game began to make more sense. Soon I found that I was able to anticipate where my opponents would be on the field. In one year, I began to learn (and enjoy) the game. I had worked through those feelings of inadequacy. I hadn't quit. I was beginning to prove to myself that I might have a future in football.

MY UNDERDOG STORY

What do people see when they look at someone like me?

Maybe they see a former defensive end (and sometime linebacker) who played four seasons in the NFL with three different teams.

Perhaps they see an analyst on the NFL Network's top-rated show, *NFL Fantasy Live*, where I tell fantasy owners everywhere how to win their week.

Maybe they see the cohost of NBC's hit show *American Ninja Warrior*, the guy who's screaming his head off for every one of the hundreds of competitors who appear on the show each season.

They see someone successful. They see someone who has made it. They see someone who has achieved his dreams.

It's easy to see greatness in others; it's hard to see it in ourselves. Too many of us never see it at all. But it's what we see in ourselves that so often determines what we do. Almost all of us at one point in our lives dreamed of something just a little bit bigger only to have the very next thought be: *But I'm not good enough*. And like the closing of a great iron gate, those words would present a seemingly unpassable barrier between us and that dream. I can't tell you how many times I've spoken those words myself.

We see what we want in others. But when we look at ourselves, we see frailty, limits, and insecurities. It's hard to get past that image of ourselves. We want to see someone great, someone who's confident, disciplined, and determined to succeed. But it seems like a fantasy. It's not real. *Greatness?* That's a term for other people.

Greatness wasn't for me either. I wasn't supposed to have come this far. But since I have come this far, I know that I've always been the underdog.

Underdogs aren't supposed to win. For me, my story started with my parents, who came to this country with nothing. They never made much more than nothing, but they made enough to support seven children, send several to college, and raise two NFL athletes. That wasn't supposed to happen for them, and yet it did.

It would have been simpler to do the easy thing and give in to my surroundings. Joining a gang, skipping school, dealing drugs—these were all ways we could have fit in and become more

American. As it was, we weren't good enough for our peers. Underdogs aren't good enough, remember? They can't win because the odds are too large to overcome. But that's why I see myself as the underdog. I went out and competed anyway.

I learned to embrace the vision I had of myself as the underdog, as the kid who's not supposed to win. I would make it. I would get out. I would show them all that I was good enough. It's important to remember that I was never the greatest, certainly not in athletics. But I was able to improve so that I was *good enough*. I was *good enough* to make the varsity basketball team. I was *good enough* at football to get noticed by several Division I schools.

All of us, at some point in our lives, face a nearly insurmountable obstacle, and our first thought is: *I can't do it*. Sometimes these obstacles are ones we didn't choose. Life comes at you and you must either get through it or fail. You must find a way. But to be great you must keep on trying. That's what the ninjas on the show have done, and it's why you'll read about many of them in the pages that follow—the ones who have inspired me, the ones who make me feel I need to work harder, live better, and keep fighting.

By embracing my status as the underdog, I found that fire to push myself. If I was going to make it out of South Central, I had to defy the odds. My father might have forced me to play football because I had given my word, but I soon came to embrace the game as another avenue of escape. Make no mistake, I was still committed to basketball, but I had overcome my rejection of this other sport. Whatever it took, I would do. To take those reps that the better kids didn't. To stay later on the court or the field than the better kids did. To give up my free time. While the other guys played, I worked. I hustled. You should too. If you're pursuing the right dream, then it shouldn't come easy. Others shouldn't expect you to accomplish it. Use those low expectations to light that fire in your belly. Embrace your role as an underdog. Get ready to show them—more importantly, yourself—that you deserve to be there.

MY NAME IS AKBAR GBAJABIAMILA

Part of being an underdog is going after something even that others think is ridiculous. They can't understand why someone *like you* would waste your time on it. "*American Ninja Warrior?* Are you kidding me?" Often, it's that little bit of "reality check" that keeps us from going after what we really want. "You're right. It's a silly idea. I'd never get on *American Ninja Warrior.*" And just like that, the dream is dead.

You don't need to be a black kid from South Central LA to accept the limits others put on you. We do it all the time. Even when I was out of the NFL and trying to pursue a career in broadcasting, I fought against the limits others wanted to put on me. I came very close to believing them, and it nearly broke me.

When we listen to others tell us what we should do, what we can't do, and what we're nuts for even thinking about doing, we kill that dream inside us. The problem is that there's a part of us that *wants* to believe the limits others put on us. If someone says we can't do something, a lot of us feel a sense of relief. Accepting limits removes the burden of achieving our dreams. It's so much easier to live an unremarkable life, to accept our place in the world, and to think that greatness is for others, but not for us.

There's comfort in a crowd, safety in anonymity. If you don't set high goals, then no one will tell you that you're nuts. Had I walked away from football that day and gone back to what I knew and loved, I would have felt much better. My father pushed me back out. I made it to the NFL because my father wouldn't let me quit. He forced me to confront that kid I saw in the mirror each morning, the kid who hated this new, barbaric sport, who everyone expected such great things from but who couldn't move, couldn't tackle, and just flat-out couldn't play.

Don't be ashamed of who you are and what you want to accomplish. To others, it might sound crazy, absurd, a waste of time. But knowing what you want to do is part of knowing who you are. If you deny yourself that, then you will never get past seeing that insecure, timid person in the mirror who believes they aren't good enough.

When my father told me to "make them say your name," what he really meant was: "Make them see who you are." If you let your friends get away with not seeing you, then how can you handle the world? Show them that you exist. Show them that you are strong, proud, and ready. Even if you don't feel like any of those things, it doesn't matter: Make them say your name.

When we as the underdogs take on the goals that scare us, that we don't feel ready for, that others tell us we're nuts for trying, we are telling the world to say our name. When we choose the hard road, we are telling the world who we are. When we accept the task of pursuing our dreams with every ounce of our being, we are screaming that here we stand, ready to fight.

Make them say your name. Make them see you. Make them know that you are great.

My name is Akbar Oluwakemi-Idowu Gbajabiamila.

THE FIRST WOMAN

When I first saw Kacy Catanzaro step onto the course during the 2013 Venice Qualifiers, I wasn't terribly impressed. Kacy stands exactly five feet tall and weighs under a hundred pounds. Big-frame bodies don't typically do well on the *Ninja* course, for the same reason they don't make good gymnasts. To have to carry that much weight, even if it is mostly muscle, works against you. But Kacy seemed to be stretching the idea that small people make great ninjas a bit far. Sure, Kacy had been a gymnast at Towson University and had been named Southeast Regional Gymnast of the Year in 2012. Clearly, she was a good athlete, but a ninja?

I should've known that Kacy had heard it all before. Her whole life she has battled doubts because of her size. "I've always been the underdog and underestimated," she told me. In fact, the very thoughts I had when she stepped onto the course were prejudices Kacy had heard from hundreds of others. I admit it: I prejudged her, just like everyone else had.

"In gymnastics, people would always comment on my height," she says. "They'd say things like, 'You'll be good because you don't have much weight to hold up.' They didn't mean for it to sound condescending, but I was tired of everyone talking about my size. Others were just clueless. They would look at me and say, 'Oh, gosh, you're so cute.' Like I was a kid trying on an oversized coat."

Growing up with an older sister had fueled Kacy's competitive edge. During a casual softball game when she was eighteen, Kacy's mom had to remind her that they "were here to have fun." I never learned what caused her mom to say that, but, knowing Kacy, I can only imagine. Although she quickly took up gymnastics, Kacy had always been in love with obstacle training. As a child, she would watch the Japanese version of *Ninja Warrior*, which would air on the G4 cable network, mesmerized by the athletic gifts of the competitors.

She found gymnastic success in college at Towson. In addition to her Southeast Regional honors, she had also been named the 2012 Eastern College Athletic Conference Gymnast of the Year. But when she graduated, she said she felt a bit lost. How does someone with Kacy's competitive drive thrive in the working world?

"I had this feeling: 'What am I to do now? What am I training for?'" she said. One day she was resting on the couch, recovering from ankle surgery, and watching an episode of *American Ninja Warrior*. Someone on the show made a comment that caused Kacy's ears to prick up—and her competitive spirit to soar.

"I heard, 'No woman has ever completed the course.'"

When I joined in 2013, there certainly was this idea that it was "good enough" if a woman ninja made it to a certain point. The presumption was that *every* woman would eventually fall. We were all waiting for the one female competitor to break the glass ceiling.

On the couch that day, her ankle all bandaged up, Kacy decided she would be that woman.

At the 2013 Venice Qualifiers, Kacy competed—and fell. Before her run, Kacy admits, she let her doubts get the better of her. There was a jump off a trampoline on the fifth obstacle. Kacy knew she would need to jump as far as she ever had—and that this time her size was working against her. What made things worse was *others* telling her just how far she would need to jump. Again and again. The constant yammering made her question her own abilities. She knew she could make that jump, only she didn't. But what happened next changed her life.

Drying off after getting out of the pool, someone said to her: "Kacy, you did really good for a girl."

"I remember thinking, 'What in the world does that mean?'" Kacy told me. "A girl's 'good' wasn't as good as a man's 'good.' I'm not okay with that. That's something I'm going to change.

"That was a moment for me that could've gone either way," she says. "I could've believed them and been happy with being 'good for a girl.' Maybe that's the best I'll ever be. And if so, then maybe I'm not good enough to complete the course."

Or . . .

"I didn't accept it. Women *can* do this. I'm not going to settle. Right there, still feeling all the adrenaline from doing the course, the disappointment, I made a decision: *Oh, I'm going to be back here.*"

Kacy vowed then and there, still wet from the pool and still stinging from failure, that she would come back. Not only that, but she would be the first woman to complete the course. *I'm going to be good, period*, she remembers thinking.

Kacy went back to Texas and started over. She trained at the Alpha Warrior gym in San Antonio, surrounded by a close circle of family and friends, which included *Ninja* competitor and fan favorite Brent Steffensen. She credits Brent's training and influence for improving her performance. She said she felt like she was a kid again, chasing her sister. "Brent was better than me, and I was trying to catch up to him." Other than Brent, the community of ninjas who trained at the gym pushed Kacy to get better. But they also helped her overcome her doubts.

She was an underdog again, and she thrived in that role. "I'm going to prove everyone wrong."

At the Dallas Qualifiers in 2014, Kacy became the first woman to make it up the Warped Wall. And when she hit the buzzer, clocking in a time of 5:26.18, she became the first woman in the show's history to complete the qualifying course. But she wasn't done. The next night, Kacy broke the glass ceiling again by becoming the first—and only—woman to beat a city finals course.

Kacy continued to compete on the show for the next three years before joining WWE as a wrestler. (Yes, you read that right, Mighty Kacy is a professional wrestler today.) I asked her about continuing with competition even after she had done more than any other woman had done.

She told me: "When I really thought about why I loved doing *American Ninja Warrior*, I realized that it wasn't the winning that kept me going; it was those moments where I could be that change for people. When a little girl comes up to me at the grocery store and excitedly says that she wants to do what I do; when an older man told me that I inspired him to lead a healthier, more active life—it's those moments when I knew I had touched people's lives and made a difference. Those are the moments that I really love. A lot of the women who have surpassed my achievements on the show have said to me: 'I saw your run and that inspired me.' Now those women are inspiring others. It's a ripple effect. Women are breaking boundaries; we're going further."

When I first saw Kacy Catanzaro, I saw someone who I didn't think was strong enough. She was an underdog from the moment she made the vow to be as good as any man on the show, to be equal with the male competitors. She saw herself as an underdog, but she also thrived in that role. Kacy wanted to prove to everyone that she belonged. And that's how she became the first. Now, when people say the name of Kacy Catanzaro, they say the name of a woman who made the world pay attention.

2

REJECT YOUR CIRCUMSTANCES

When I was just a boy, I would go to my mother's salon after school to watch TV. She had a store on a busy street in South Central with a big metal gate that she would pull down to protect it at night.

One day when I was in the sixth grade, a man walks in and asks my mother if the store is open. The television was near the front door, behind a counter, and I turn my head, because the voice sounds strange. The next thing I hear is the man saying, "Give me your money!" That makes me turn around and I see the man holding a gun to my mother's head. She grabs the money out of the register in wads and puts it in the bag the man is holding out. He then turns to leave, but catches a glimpse of me sitting there. He has every reason to run out the door, only he doesn't.

Instead, he walks toward me, raises his gun, and points it at my head.

"Please," I hear my mother whimper, "please, take me."

The man doesn't speak, and I am too scared to do anything except stare down the barrel of that gun. He holds it at my face for a moment longer, then leaves. That is it. I watch him run across four lanes of traffic, dodging the cars, hoping that one would hit him. None do. In fact, no one does anything. Just another day in the hood.

The next day I went back to school. Sure, I was traumatized. Sure, I wanted to hide under my bed and never leave. But when you have known kids and adults who have been gunned down, your story just isn't all that special. It was routine. That was life in South Central Los Angeles in the 1980s and 1990s.

Not long after, in 1992, Los Angeles erupted in riots, triggered by the acquittal of the police officers who had beaten Rodney King. I say LA, but to be more precise, it was my neighborhood of South Central. By this point, I was in the seventh grade and understood that I lived in a dangerous neighborhood, but the riots weren't something anyone could prepare for. Flames soon engulfed my whole world. I mean, literally. During the height of the riots, with fires raging all around us, my parents had us spray the roof of our two-story house with an old garden hose to keep it wet. Up there on the balcony, we could see nothing but burning buildings in all directions. Papa's Grocery Store was in flames, and so was the 48th Street Market, both right down the street. The looters weren't discriminating. They burned black-owned businesses as well as Korean businesses. I remember thinking, *If they're mad, go burn down Beverly Hills.*

A lot of my friends—and their parents—went out looting. You knew because they showed up to school with brand-new clothes after the riots. But our parents kept us in the house, which infuriated me at the time. We needed so much, and it was all right there for the taking. We didn't even have a couch. But no, my parents didn't believe in stealing. That was that.

I can still see the tanks rolling down the street in front of my mother's salon, and the National Guard soldiers with their machine guns. My parents had talked to us about the civil war that had gripped Nigeria in their childhoods, and now I was seeing something similar. The city implemented a curfew, which we kids didn't like, but school was also shut down for two weeks because the air was so full of ash. We looked at it like a vacation. Two weeks of TV and no homework.

To say that the world in which I grew up was an obstacle for me is a bit of an understatement. Looking back, I'm still amazed at how I survived, much less overcame those conditions to find success. I credit my parents, my siblings, and those who held out their hands to me. If I was unlucky in the place and circumstances of my childhood, I was extremely blessed in whom God chose as my parents, as well as the others who loved me.

We can't choose a lot of what happens to us in life, particularly when we're young. Kids believe that the world around them is the only world that exists. Circumstances that would defeat an adult just bounce right off a resilient kid. I didn't know how crazy my circumstances were until I was much older, probably a teenager. By then I had come to realize that, while I was proud of where I was from, I didn't want to stay there. I wanted to get out and find a better life.

A lot of professional athletes come from humble beginnings. In such a world, a child learns to use his athletic talents. Athletics not only gave us joy and purpose in life, it could also be our ticket out of our circumstances. However, you don't need to be from the hood to experience terrible circumstances. I can't imagine what yours might be, but I know there's something—perhaps many things—in your life holding you back.

I could have easily blamed my circumstances for my failures in life. If I hadn't made it to San Diego State, I would've been labeled one of the guys who didn't make it out. I could have said I didn't have the support; that I had to dodge bullets; that I had parents who, though loving and supportive, fought like crazy in front of us kids.

The life around me was the only life I had ever known. My parents did their best to expose me to a better life, a life outside South Central, and probably for this reason above all others, I was able to expand my horizons and dream differently than many of my peers. My brother Kabeer's success as a high school athlete, which led to a scholarship to San Diego State University, also helped broaden my mind and harden my resolve.

So when I finally did get out of the hood, I was able to look back and ask: Was it pure luck? Was I just the fortunate one with two parents who showed me a better life ahead? Yes, but that's not the whole story. The story wouldn't be complete without *my* involvement in it. I *could* have taken my parents' loving home and sound wisdom and turned away from it like a know-it-all youth. I *could* have chosen to follow some of my friends into the poor life choices of the street.

After all, when I walked out the door each day, leaving my parents behind, there were a thousand different bad decisions before me that were easier than to try to live like a normal, law-abiding, sober teenager. The choices I could have made were the ones my world asked me to accept as inevitable.

You don't need school, so just skip it.

You're going to have to fight for everything, so you'd better learn on the streets.

The white man doesn't want us to succeed, so just give up.

It is by accepting the excuses of your circumstances that you immediately limit your potential—or destroy it. Away from my home and parents, my circumstances growing up were defined by the hood. With few isolated exceptions, my circumstances wanted me to believe that there was no way out. And if there's no way out, then why bother?

WE HAVE THE POWER

My desire to leave the hood says nothing about how much I love where I'm from. I'm proud of it, as much as I'm proud of being Nigerian. There's a certain bond that connects folks from the hood. Even in the way that someone says it—"I'm from the hood, from the h to the d"—you can tell how much a person went through.

Yet there's a fine line between pride and acceptance. You can be proud that you're from the hood, but to accept it as your lot in life from which there is no escape is dangerous. From a very young age, I had to walk that line between pride and acceptance. I didn't see it that way at the time, of course. I'd say that I was tempted by the hood's false idols. When you grow up with next to nothing, the kid in your class sporting the new shoes and the legit jersey seems like he has it all. We value the wrong things as children. Even though my parents tried (and succeeded) in steering my and my siblings' eyes toward what was truly important in life, you can't stop a kid from being covetous. And I was insanely envious of the guys around me who showed off the things they had.

In the seventh grade, my friend John Terrell had a fresh pair of Jordan 4s. He said he'd let me wear them since he knew I'd never be able to get a pair of my own. Of course, I knew how John got those Jordans, and it wasn't with money from a job or his parents. John was part of a posse, NBT (or "Nothin' But Trouble"). Posses are the entry point to gangs, and as such they prey on kids in junior high. That doesn't make them any less dangerous, but the usual way of a gangbanger was to join a posse when he was in grade school, then get hazed into one of the gangs, like the Crips or the Bloods.

My father had talked to me about gangs, and I had enough sense to know I shouldn't be in one. But, boy, I liked John's Jordans. He knew that too and asked me to join NBT. It was a terrible temptation for me, one that so many of my friends had failed to overcome. The desire to belong, to fit in, is powerful for any child, but for me it was nearly irresistible. Growing up, I had been teased relentlessly for my Nigerian heritage. Around the fourth or fifth grade, I tried to turn the tables on my tormenters to shield myself from them. I would talk about all the money I had, and how I had flown to school in a helicopter. Everyone knew I was lying, but they loved my amazingly ridiculous stories.

On the playground, I would gather a crowd around me and slam my head into the tetherball pole. Why? Probably because it took the focus off my name and clothes and put it on something else they could laugh at. And I would say, my head stinging and ringing, "You Americans are all so weak!" The kids would howl, and that's what I wanted. If they were laughing at me for banging my head against a pole, then they weren't laughing at me for my cheap Converse shoes, which were definitely not in style back then. (We called them "Gumbys.")

The flip side of the coin is that someone can be disowned by the hood. You have to think of the hood like a small town, where everybody knows your business. It's easy to get a reputation and even easier to have everyone know about it. My father had a good reputation as an honest man and hardworking plumber. If you were part of a gang, everyone knew about it too. The ones who were disowned were those who spoke a certain way or acted a certain way (speak "white" and act "white" is how it went). Former gang members were also disowned, if not killed. For those who don't know what it's like to live in a small-town community like that, there's a tremendous amount of pressure to fit in. Those who don't are in danger, and some are forced to leave altogether. I knew guys who left the gangs whose parents had to move them away. It was either that or live in constant fear.

Temptation. Belonging. Fear. That's how the gangs get you. It's how the hood moves you closer to acceptance, that the hand you were dealt is the one you must keep. I nearly gave in too. I might have. My mind told me that I should stay as far away from posses and gangs as I could. So I told John that I would think about his offer, but in my heart, I wanted to have what he had. I was fortunate, though. Somehow word got around that I was thinking about joining NBT and my older brother and sister, who were in the ninth grade at the time, heard about it. Then they told my father.

When I got home one evening, my father confronted me. "You want to be a gangbanger?" I tried to deny everything, but he wasn't having it. I got a whooping that night, and it might have saved my life. I didn't join NBT. (I was still more afraid of my father than not fitting in.) Not long after that I was supposed to meet John at his locker so he would let me wear his Jordans, but he never showed up. That day during science class, our teacher, Mr. McInerny, told us that John had been shot and killed. It was the first time I had lost someone close to me.

The idea of gang life just got real. It wasn't about materialism or respect; it was about your life. My parents helped us reject our circumstances in other ways too. They did so by introducing us to successful people, professionals with higher degrees. PhDs, MDs, master's, etc. I can still hear my father: "Are you going to get your master's?" Or the way he pronounced PhD: "P *hech* D." The one imperative I heard from my father time and again growing up was "Learn a trade!" He meant it in the sense of what he and my mother did—plumbing and hairdressing—but he also meant it in the academic sense. Lawyers, doctors, engineers—these were "trade" professions. They required additional schooling. My mother used her salon as a hub for gossip and information. She was the consummate networker and would have customers from all walks of life. When they sat down in her chair, she would get them talking: "My husband is a doctor . . ." "I am a lawyer . . ." To us kids, they were complete strangers, but to my parents, these were the people who had lived the American Dream. They were successful because they had an education.

Despite living in the hood, my parents had the perspective only immigrants can have. They wanted us to be thankful for what we had, as little as it seemed to us then. They would regale us with stories about life back in Nigeria, about the poverty, the constant civil wars, and the corrupt officials who battled each other for control of the country. Meanwhile, the people suffered, living in horrendous conditions. My father would always scold us for leaving the faucet on. It didn't make any sense. Who cared if we wasted a little bit of water? But he would tell us how in his village back in Nigeria he had to walk a mile to fetch water from the well. Every drop was as priceless as an ounce of gold. When that's *your* childhood, South Central LA seems like Beverly Hills.

"You don't know nothing," my parents would tell us. "We'll take you to Nigeria."

We never believed the threat, but their message did sink in. We understood at some level that our parents came from much worse than what we were going through. We wanted Guess jeans; they had wanted running water and constant electricity. We had thick heads, but the lesson got through. The people they introduced us to showed us that there is a life beyond the hood. A whole world, in fact, where education and hard work are valued and rewarded. We were still kids, and I certainly had my moments of coveting others' possessions, but we saw and we heard.

And we wanted out. At least I did. Because of my parents' influence and my own experiences, I saw that to accept my circumstances would be a betrayal of everything that my parents had sacrificed and worked toward. I was in the ninth grade when this realization hit me. Our home was the largest and on a corner lot, but it was always in disrepair. I mean literally. My parents had a bunch of unfinished renovation projects that left the house looking like it was under construction: plywood walls outside, unfinished drywall on the inside. We kids were embarrassed to have our friends come over. In fact, we had them drop us off a few doors down, telling the mother or father who was driving that *this* was our house, just to avoid the humiliation of them seeing the real one.

Then, when I was a freshman, I dared to have a friend over. I regretted it instantly. He pointed at everything and laughed. "You have pay phone!" (We did—it took quarters.) "You ain't got no carpet!" (We didn't.) I couldn't say anything. Instead, I vowed there and then that I would do better. I would make something of myself so that I could be proud of where I lived. Looking at this now, I realize that this might sound disrespectful to my parents, who did what they could to provide the seven of us with a home. But then I remember where *they* came from, and I realize that my thoughts were no different from theirs when they looked at the state of affairs in Nigeria and wanted out.

South Central was better than Nigeria, yes; but there were still brighter horizons for us. I didn't see it this way at the time, but now I realized that to get out, we first had to reject our circumstances. We had to reject the idea that we had no power over the life outside (and sometimes inside) our door.

It's hard to reject your circumstances when you think you're not good enough. Even today, I have to consciously rid my mind of doubt when I strive for something new. I'm sure much of this is just part of who I am, but I can also trace it to my childhood. Growing up the way I did left a lasting impression. Watching TV, reading the newspapers, it was clear that the rest of the country didn't expect anything of people who lived in the hood. Is it any wonder so many turned to gangs? In a gang, a kid can find purpose, meaning, friendship. In a gang, a kid is someone. In return, the gang gives the kid a feeling of power and authority. Other people are afraid of you. And that is a very empowering feeling to have.

The temptations put before us asked us to accept this reality as the only one possible. If I were to break free, I not only had to refuse the temptations, I had to see them for what they were:

chains to keep me from using my gifts and striving toward that purpose God had for me. These temptations can often appear small—a pair of Jordans!—but they are immediate. They are right in front of us. Our dreams, those brighter horizons, must be worked toward to be realized. And so many of us take the temptations, not because we don't want to break free, but because they're so easy to take. And when we do, we move that much closer to acceptance.

Even though I flirted with joining NBT, I quickly overcame those temptations and stayed gang-free. I understand why so many kids, desperate for a sense of belonging, of purpose, choose the dangerous life of the gangs. They see no way out. Even if they can imagine a world outside the hood, they don't think they have a chance at it.

And once we start gobbling up those temptations and lifestyle traps, we start to lose control over our lives. We start to believe we have no power over these outside forces. For me, I struggled constantly to overcome the false ideas society had placed on me.

I'm not smart enough.

I'm too African.

I won't make it to eighteen.

I don't have the raw talent.

My parents can't afford college.

You know what else these circumstances are? Excuses.

I learned eventually that I did have power over these circumstances. I didn't have to accept them as limiting. It required tons of hard work, but so often we don't even bother with the work. We think we can't do it. That we're powerless.

Look at your own circumstances and think about how you're letting them limit you. Whatever excuses you're accepting as inevitable, cast them into the sea. Cast them far away from you so that you can confidently walk toward your dream.

GIVE YOURSELF GRACE

My first year of football was a disaster. I didn't want to be there, and the coaches knew I didn't want to be there. In fact, one evening after practice, my coach caught me shooting hoops in the gym. It seemed harmless enough to me, but to him, it meant that I really didn't care that much about my football game. He slammed the door on me. If I had time and energy to practice my jumper, then I had time and energy to practice hitting the gaps. I also had a bad attitude. You know, the attitude of an entitled teenager. Coach was right to keep me on the bench.

But I got better. More important, I stuck to it. In high school, I never really grasped the game on a deeper level. I was a large body who learned where he needed to go. But after not starting a single game as a junior, I was finally named a starter my senior year. That, combined with my rising talent, had me focus more and more on football. Improvement followed. Then, during my senior year, I started to receive scholarship offers. I still barely understood the game, but colleges look a lot at potential when recruiting. They saw my size and athleticism, and even though I couldn't tell you the difference between a 3–4 or a 4–3, my brother's success at San Diego State told the scouts that I had football talent *somewhere* in me.

I had interest from the University of California, Berkeley; Oregon; Fresno State; and Colorado State. But I chose San Diego State University, mostly because it was close to home and that's where my brother went. Who better to show me the way to gridiron excellence than my brother? Like a kid emulating his big brother, I would do what he did. I would *be like Kabeer*.

Of course, this made any success I had on the field relative to my brother's success. And the simple fact was that I wasn't as good as Kabeer. After being redshirted as a freshman, Kabeer was an immediate starter. I had to fight my way into the starting lineup. Even as my brother left college for the NFL, I was chasing him, desperately trying to re-create the success he had seen on the field as the school's all-time sack leader. It was obvious, however, that I wasn't my brother.

The frustration began to mount. The question—"How come you don't play like Kabeer?"—was like a dagger in my heart every time I heard it. I wasn't good enough and I would never be good enough. It's crazy how our minds can reach such preposterous conclusions based on so little evidence. Had I put my faith in God, rather than my terribly imperfect powers of prediction, then I might have been able to take a breath and continue working. But it took a conversation with my defensive line coach, Ken Delgado, that year to snap me back to reality.

"Akbar," he started, "can a lion run as fast as a cheetah?"

"No, Coach."

"And can a cheetah fight like a lion?"

"Nope."

"Then listen," he said, looking directly at me, "your brother is a cheetah and you're a lion. Stop trying to run like a cheetah. Fight like the lion you are."

It was an instant change. At six feet, four inches tall and 218 pounds, Kabeer was the cheetah because of his ridiculous speed and agility. He had honed his game to make the best use of those gifts. I was six feet six and 245 pounds, nearly thirty pounds heavier than him! Of course I couldn't be like Kabeer. Comparing myself to my brother had gotten me this far—I was on a scholarship to a Division I football school—but the level I was now playing at demanded more. It demanded that I stop chasing my brother, trying to be more like him. As my coaches saw, by trying to be something I wasn't, I wasn't playing as well as I could.

So I stopped chasing my brother. I let my cheetah brother go. I started to run my own race, as a lion. That's when everything started to change.

We live in a world where everything has to happen *now*. We expect immediate results. We want immediate success. We lose interest when life doesn't happen on our schedule. So we turn to a different sport or a different dream. When that doesn't happen, we turn to another. And another. We end up never succeeding at anything because we left before the miracle could happen. We left before our hard work could pay off. By the time I entered college I had been playing football for two years. Two years! Kabeer had been playing almost his entire adolescence. Yet I wanted what he had. I just didn't want to have to wait for it. When success didn't happen on my timetable, I let my old feelings of inadequacy—of not being good enough—convince me that I would *never* be good enough.

But I am reminded today that success, like God, doesn't abide by our schedules. He works on His own time, and success finds us when we've earned it. We must exercise patience, not jump to conclusions that reflect our lack of confidence more than they reflect the facts. The facts were that I needed to learn a lot more about the game of football before I could hope to match Kabeer. As it would turn out, I never matched my brother. But I became my own player. I developed my own game. And I did so when I stopped expecting something to happen immediately.

I developed patience, and, more important, I learned how to give myself grace. When we try to manipulate success to meet our purposes, we put unrealistic expectations on ourselves. For someone who was already hard on himself, my attempt to be a great football star before I was ready nearly drove me from the game. When success doesn't happen quickly, we start to doubt ourselves. Doubt leads to insecurity. We want to throw in the towel. We're reminded of what everyone said about our dream. It's silly. It's impossible. It's not for us. Then we start to believe we're not good enough. And that's when we quit.

When I learned to give myself grace, I stopped being so hard on myself. I allowed myself to be not good enough. I started to enjoy the game and learn to love my role in it. Then success started to happen. The hard work began to pay off.

That doesn't mean success is supposed to happen. But when you give yourself grace, when you allow yourself to accept your weaknesses and failings, then you can accept what happens, good or bad, more easily. I'm not saying any of this is easy, but we too often fall prey to the mind-set that all that's required to succeed is rock-solid determination and hard work. Nowhere in this book will you find me singling out "hard work" as a core lesson. That's because hard work is obvious. You don't need me to tell you to work hard.

What you might need me to tell you is what to do when all your hard work has yielded little in the way of results. *That's* the dangerous moment. *That's* when you might quit. *That's* when you need to look squarely at the facts and ask yourself if you've given enough time for success to happen. Or are you putting unrealistic expectations on yourself?

God has given us all His grace, whether we work for it or not. We should learn from Him and give ourselves some too.

"WHAT'S YOUR EXCUSE?"

Jimmy Choi was a forty-two-year-old family man from Illinois when he appeared in Season 9 during the Kansas City Qualifiers of *American Ninja Warrior*. A viewer who might have had the sound turned off on his television would have seen a fit, middle-aged man performing well.

A more perceptive viewer might have noticed that Jimmy's right hand trembled throughout his run or that his jersey blared "Team

Fox" across the chest. That's because Jimmy Choi has Parkinson's disease, a progressive neurodegenerative disorder for which there is no cure.

I was no stranger to Parkinson's. My father was diagnosed with the disease when I was in college, and I have had to watch, horrified, a once strong and proud man slowly wither. So when Jimmy Choi stepped up to the podium, I was touched, but skeptical. My first thought was, *I hope this dude doesn't hurt himself.* I thought it would be a great achievement if Jimmy got past the first obstacle, but I figured he wouldn't get much farther than that.

I was already making excuses for Jimmy Choi, a man I didn't know and whose circumstances I could only superficially understand. After all, everything I knew about Parkinson's told me that Jimmy wouldn't get far, and that he probably shouldn't be on the course in the first place.

I might have known a bit about Parkinson's, but I didn't know Jimmy Choi. He made it to the third obstacle—a rotating pipe bridge that twisted along its axis when one attempted to run across. Into the pool Jimmy went. In doing so, Jimmy proved me wrong. But he did more than that: Jimmy inspired me in a way few others in my life have done.

Jimmy was diagnosed with early-onset Parkinson's when he was just twenty-seven—fifteen years before he walked to the starting line of *American Ninja Warrior*. When he received his diagnosis, Jimmy was told he would be in a wheelchair by the time he was forty. Two years after that deadline, he was competing on one of the most physically challenging shows ever created.

Perhaps training for fifteen years would give anyone, even someone suffering such a debilitating disease like Parkinson's, the strength, endurance, and confidence to get on that course and complete two obstacles. Except that's not Jimmy's story.

When he was given his diagnosis, Jimmy said he went into denial. "I believed that I had maybe ten working years left," and then he would be useless to his family. So, at first, he went into overdrive at work, doing his best to earn enough to make up for the long, dark years when he would be bound to a wheelchair. Otherwise, he ignored his disease.

"I took a pill and that was it," Jimmy told me. "I never went back to the doctors and I never upgraded my medication. I never learned about Parkinson's beyond what I was told that day in the doctor's office."

As one would expect, Jimmy's symptoms progressed. He would come home from work bone-tired, unable to experience the joys of a growing family. His physical condition worsened to the point that Jimmy, once a multisport athlete, gave up exercise. He gained weight rapidly. For eight years he lived like this, his body progressively deteriorating and always that clock ticking down to his fortieth year.

"I stopped doing any physical activity because I would always lose my balance," he says. "Six years after my diagnosis, I weighed 240 pounds and was walking with a cane."

After his son was born in 2009, Jimmy was holding him as he attempted to walk down the stairs in his home. He tripped. Somehow, he managed to protect his infant boy from injury, but

he found himself at the bottom of the stairs, his wife and oldest daughter looking over him, crying.

"It was then," he says, "lying on my back, my wife wondering if she should call an ambulance, that I knew I had reached the critical moment: I could either throw in the towel, or I could get up and do something about it."

Jimmy got off the floor.

His early efforts of doing "something about it" were educational. He began to learn about this terrible disease that rarely attacks someone as young as he was. He read up on the efforts to find a cure, only to come to the grim realization that there wasn't one on the horizon. That led Jimmy to clinical trials. He effectively gave his body over to science for a time, letting doctors and scientists use him like a lab rat in their quest for answers.

The trials never led to a miracle pill, but Jimmy did learn a lot from them. "Every trial I took part in, I noticed, had a physical component," he says. "They wanted to see how my body reacted physically both before and after the administration of the experimental treatment."

But Jimmy also noticed how well he felt after that short bout of physical activity. In fact, as he learned from the researchers, the *only* thing that seems to halt or slow Parkinson's progression is physical activity. The news was both a revelation and a tragedy. Finally, Jimmy had found an answer that, if not a cure, was at least a promise that he had some control. He didn't have to accept being an invalid before he was an invalid. At the same time, he

looked back on eight years of denial, depression, and near-total inactivity and regretted his "lost years."

Still, it wasn't hopeless, not anymore. He finally realized he had more power over his circumstances than he had ever imagined.

Jimmy started to take daily walks around his house, with a cane and his wife nearby for support. One lap turned to two, then three.

"My balance came back," says Jimmy. "Those walks became my new drug."

Fueled by the results, Jimmy went further. He extended his walks to a half-mile, then a mile, then a mile and a half. Jimmy's mantra soon became: "To do more today than I did yesterday." Before long, he had started jogging, then running. Every morning, every day.

A few months later, Jimmy was on a plane headed toward a business meeting. He found an issue of *Runner's World* in the seat pocket and flipped through it. And there he saw a story about a runner with Parkinson's who had run a marathon. The moment Jimmy got back home he told his wife he was going to run a 5K. This wasn't just a worthy goal for a guy with Parkinson's; pre-Parkinson's Jimmy had never run more than a mile and a half. In other words, Jimmy wanted to do more than he ever had.

When he crossed that finish line, Jimmy did so to the cries and screams of his family. And even though the training had been remarkable for his health, Jimmy was conflicted. "All I had done was run a 5K," he told me. "It shouldn't have been such a big deal. No other runner had a cheering section like I had."

Grace, Jimmy. Give yourself some grace.

A month after the 5K he ran a 10K; a month later, a 15K. Meanwhile, Jimmy noticed that the episodes of trembling in between his medication intake—when a Parkinson's patient experiences the worst episodes of trembling—were growing shorter. The running was helping his body metabolize the medication faster. Jimmy decided to keep it going.

In September 2012, Jimmy ran his first half-marathon. The moment he crossed the finish line he knew he wanted to run a full marathon. The next one was in Chicago, and only a month away. The race was full, but Jimmy learned that bibs for charity were still available. He just had to find a charity that would accept him.

"That's how I first discovered Team Fox, of the Michael J. Fox Foundation," says Jimmy. "I called them, and they told me they had one bib left. To this day I feel that spot was left for me."

Jimmy completed his first marathon in four hours and twenty-six minutes. As he describes his feeling afterward, "I was hooked." Since then, Jimmy has run fifteen marathons, more than a hundred half-marathons, and even a few fifty-mile "ultra" marathons. In between the marathons, he also does triathlons, one-hundred-mile bike races, and mud runs. He's also dropped eighty pounds.

Oh, and he turned forty and there wasn't a wheelchair in sight.

"These are the things I'm able to do because I keep pushing myself," says Jimmy. "What more can I do today than I did yesterday?"

After so many long-distance runs, one might think that Jimmy would come to a point where there wasn't anything "more" he could do. But his daughter gave him something.

"She's always been a big fan of *American Ninja Warrior*," he says. "She had even started taking lessons at the local gym, performing on the obstacles herself."

And every season, Kiana would beg her father to try out. Imagine that. She should be helping Jimmy eat his food, walk to the bathroom, and get dressed. Instead, she wants to know why he won't go on *American Ninja Warrior*.

"I had plenty of excuses for her," says Jimmy. "I didn't think I had the upper-body strength. And I certainly didn't have the balance."

Then, as Jimmy and his daughter were watching the show during Season 8, a female ninja who was also disabled was profiled and competed on the course.

When the segment ended, Kiana looked at her father and asked: "What's your excuse?"

"I didn't have any, not anymore."

That's how Jimmy Choi became a ninja.

Jimmy's run affected me deeply afterward, and not just for the obvious reasons. By overcoming his tragic disease, Jimmy turned himself into a beacon of hope for everyone else who suffers from Parkinson's—or any other debilitating ailment. He did it for himself, but he also did it for *them*. Becoming part of Team Fox propelled Jimmy into the next phase of the competition. He fought for someone else, and that's why he fought so hard.

3

CLOSED MOUTHS DON'T GET FED

"Meet me after school."

Four words that seemed so trivial at the time, but, looking back, they changed my life. As I've mentioned often enough already, I loved basketball growing up, but I couldn't make a shot to save my life. Even though I was the tallest kid in my class, I was typically the last kid picked for the basketball team. Part of my problem was that I simply couldn't handle the size of my body. A lot of kids experience this before they mature fully. That doesn't make living through it any less humiliating or awkward.

My one desire in grade school was to get better at basketball. I was tired of being the "sorry kid," the one who never got picked to play, the one who walked off the court while everyone else stayed till sundown. I practiced on my own, shooting the ball by myself for hours after school. I had a good work ethic and I certainly had the determination, but it seemed like no matter what I did, nothing helped.

I met Sandy Frazier when I was thirteen years old. One day, he'd seen me on the Audubon Junior High basketball court. There I was, all alone, working on my jump shot. In my dreams, the crowd roared as I swished the ball effortlessly into the hoop.

But in real life, I didn't have a consistent shot. I told Sandy (who asked me to call him Sandy, never "Mr. Frazier") that I was trying hard to get better, but that nothing seemed to work. He must have seen the look of determination and frustration in my eyes.

"Meet me after school," he said. I did so, and from that moment on I had my own personal coach, and I never missed a session.

Our training sessions weren't limited to the basketball court. Sandy helped me understand that part of my problem was simply that, like many kids, I was growing quickly and grappling with the increasing size of my body. He was a bit like Mr. Miyagi from *The Karate Kid*, constantly using different training techniques to help me hone my skills and temper my body like a piece of iron. One day we would be practicing my jump shot, another day we would be working on strength, and then on other days we'd focus on endurance (not my favorite activity at the time), which involved driving out to the beach so we could run the Manhattan Beach sand dunes or the Santa Monica Stairs, which is a set of hundred-step stairs that descend into Los Angeles from the Santa Monica canyon.

Over the years, Sandy Frazier has served not just as a coach but also as a valued mentor and dear friend. There was no question in my mind that his coaching allowed me to make the Crenshaw High School varsity basketball team. But perhaps more important, he showed me that *a desire to make something happen is not enough*. Most goals worth achieving require tremendous focus, passion, and commitment to proper preparation.

I can't explain everything I learned from Sandy Frazier. Yes, he gave me what I had asked for: the skills to play basketball at a high level. I made the varsity team my junior year. But, looking back, he taught me more about life than he ever did about basketball. To get what you want, you must do what the best do: You must emulate them by studying them, learning their techniques, and memorizing their play style. You must work—both your body and your mind.

When I graduated high school with a scholarship to play football at San Diego State, I made sure to thank Sandy. He had given me so much; what could I do to pay him back?

"Akbar," he told me, "you owe me nothing."

I didn't get into San Diego State on athletics alone. I also had to get a certain score on the SAT. But my whole life I had struggled with test taking. (I would later learn in college that I had a processing disorder.) As it did with Sandy Frazier, basketball would provide me with another mentor. The father of a teammate of mine, Mr. Garrison, would drive us home from practice.

During my senior year, as we were walking out of the gym, Mr. Garrison mentioned that he had read an article about me and the Division I schools recruiting me to play football.

"Yes," I replied, "but my SAT scores aren't good enough yet." By this point I had taken the SAT once or twice, and my hopes for getting that Division I scholarship diminished after each one.

"Really?" Mr. Garrison said. "Why don't you come by the house tomorrow after practice and we can talk about this."

As with Sandy Frazier, I accepted Mr. Garrison's offer, which is how he became my tutor—and mentor—for the SAT. But when I say "tutor," I want to be clear about Mr. Garrison's teaching style. His wasn't a method that demanded rigorous nose-in-the-books discipline. I had that—and it wasn't working. The best way I can describe it is that Mr. Garrison discovered how a kid like me, who didn't seem to retain information when taught in the traditional manner, learned best. Just like Sandy, he would use nontraditional lessons to get me to remember my math, my history, my science, and my English. Reading information wasn't enough for me; I needed someone who could help me process what I had just read. So, for example, I'd read Socrates, and then Mr. Garrison and I would have a conversation about Socrates. He also saw that I had very little cultural awareness, by which I mean I didn't know much beyond my world of South Central. I vividly remember watching *The Cosby Show* with Mr. Garrison, who explained to me that the home the Huxtables lived in was called a brownstone. As far as I knew, there weren't any brownstones in LA, and certainly none in South Central. Funnily enough, a question on the SAT Analogies and Comparisons was: "Wood: House." The answer was: "Brick: Brownstone." I got it right, of course, but only because of Mr. Garrison.

And like Sandy, Mr. Garrison gave me what I needed. My scores on the SAT jumped dramatically, and I was accepted to SDSU. When I went to thank him and ask him if I could pay him back, he just told me to get him an Aztec football T-shirt. That's all he wanted, after all the hours he had put in with me. And so, I left the summer before my freshman year to get some course credits before school officially began. I bought Mr. Garrison that shirt and couldn't wait to give it to him. When I returned to Los Angeles at the end of the summer term, my father told me that Mr. Garrison had died.

I ran out of the house and sprinted toward Mr. Garrison's, my father following me. I reached his door and started banging on it, tears running down my face, shouting, "Mr. Garrison! Mr. Garrison!" I know now that Mr. Garrison didn't really care about a T-shirt. The shirt was just a symbol; it represented the victory *he* felt helping me get into college. My acceptance was all the thanks he needed.

Sandy Frazier and Mr. Garrison—where would we be without such people? Not only did they help me, they also inspired me to emulate their example of selflessness and mentorship.

THE HUMILITY TO ASK

The way of fools seems right to them,
but the wise listen to advice.
—*Proverbs 12:15*

Who I am, what I am, where I am, and what I do—I owe these things to those who helped me achieve them. I didn't do it alone. No one does it alone. People come into our lives who fundamentally alter our life's trajectory. Sometimes they're our parents, our friends, or our teachers, and sometimes they're strangers, put before us by God to assist us in our journey. I look back on the path I've traveled, and I see their faces, the faces of selfless men and women who decided to help a kid named Akbar.

Teenagers think they have it all figured out. It's only when we become adults that we look back on the things our parents said—the things we ignored—and realize, *You know what? They were right.* If we're lucky, we haven't made some huge mistake by having dismissed their advice. That's normal for anyone. But if we're still acting like teenagers when we're adults, if we're still ignoring the advice or offers of help because we "have it all figured out," then we are giving up on one of the greatest gifts in life: the chance to have a mentor.

In my life, I've been fortunate to have many mentors help me along the way. I hope to have many more. My hunger to learn, to improve, to achieve, didn't end with Sandy Frazier and

Mr. Garrison. If anything, they ignited within me a desire to find others just like them. By far the greatest thing they taught me is that I can't do it alone. They also probably helped me avoid that arrogant streak so common to most teenagers. I had my moments growing up, but I saw inside me the change that these men helped create.

Where does one find such people? I won't discount the role of fate in crossing paths with two remarkable individuals—and at a time in my life when I most needed them. But we don't find those we need because we're lucky. We find those we need because we have the humility to accept help when it's offered.

Accepting help. It's one of the toughest things in the world to do. There seems to be a resistance in many of us to accept or to ask for help, because we think that it represents weakness. We fear exposing our insecurities, doubts, and problems to others. We would rather fail than admit to someone that we need help.

I can handle it.

I'm fine.

I don't have a problem.

And then we wonder why we weren't *lucky enough* to have any good mentors help us through those tough moments. The truth is that those mentors were probably all around us, we just didn't ask or accept their offer. Those mentors probably offered their hand, but we just didn't see it. I am not more fortunate than others in my abundance of mentors; I just had the humility to accept and, in some cases, to ask. I didn't care how I might appear, if I looked weak or stupid. If I wanted to reach my goals, I needed help.

Who says that an underdog must do it alone? The idea that the victory of achieving your dreams is sweeter if you didn't have any help is ridiculous. The ninjas on the show compete alone. It's just them, on the course, with no help: no team, no coach. But behind each one is a long line of people who helped them get there. Some of those people might be in the stands cheering along with me. Some of them might be watching at home. And some of them might no longer be here. But they were there when the ninja needed them. And I know that, whether the course is completed or not, each ninja sees those mentors' faces when he or she finishes their run. We must reject the notion that there is something more honorable or noble in doing it all by yourself.

We cannot deny ourselves the miracle of a mentor out of fear or arrogance. I am humbled that people like Sandy and Mr. Garrison entered my life, but they weren't the only ones. The miracle isn't that mentors exist and want to help us achieve our dreams; the miracle is that there are so many willing to help—if you ask.

THE AGONY OF DOUBT

One of the most terrible places to be is stuck in your own head. If we stay up there too long, we start to imagine impending doom. We think of all the reasons we can't do something. We imagine all the ways that something we're trying to do will go wrong. We fixate on the negative, convincing ourselves that the *only possible* outcome is failure.

Or maybe that's just me.

I had always enjoyed learning. But after having to take the SAT a few times, I started to doubt my ability. I was certain that everything I had worked so hard to achieve would disappear because I wasn't smart enough.

But the things *we* know to be true aren't always the full story. Was I the best student? Absolutely not. Should I be worried about the SAT? Absolutely. But I had taken those two truths and spun them in my head into a conclusion that wasn't true. Had I stayed in my own head and not allowed in a different viewpoint, then I would have been bound by my own limited beliefs. It took Mr. Garrison to get me thinking along different lines. It took someone else to help me put those doubts I had into their proper place. The doubts were real. But they didn't point to failure; they pointed to the fact that I needed help.

A mentor doesn't just teach you the things you need to learn to accomplish your dreams. They give you another perspective— a balanced perspective, especially when you've tied yourself into nervous knots. A mentor is there to help ease our doubts. Their presence in your life—their willingness to help—helps you remember that the things *you know to be true* might not be.

After the 1992 riots in Los Angeles, pretty much the whole country had a negative opinion about South Central. Those of us who were kids at the time were caught in the middle—on one side was the smoldering wreckage of our neighborhood, and on the other side was the belief, expressed on television and newspapers, that we would never amount to anything. The media used terms like "thug" and "hoodlum" to describe the people in my community.

Right around then a businesswoman named Melinda Mc-Mullen had a novel idea. A public-relations executive who was from LA, McMullen had watched, horrified, while her city burned. When it was over, she wondered what she could do. She would eventually meet Tammy Bird, a biology teacher at Crenshaw High School who had started asking students to help her clear a devastated lot behind her classroom and restore the garden that once grew there. Together, they came up with Food from the 'Hood, a nonprofit organization that was entirely student-run. As a business, Food from the 'Hood started selling organically grown produce from the restored garden, but in time the students, with Melinda's help, expanded into making salad dressing. The story was picked up by the press and went national. *Newsweek* gave Food from the 'Hood its American Achievement Award, complete with a front-page photo spread, and even Prince Charles showed up at Crenshaw to see what was going on. I will never forget the prince taking a bite of salad, with our dressing dripping off the lettuce, and saying, in his impeccable English accent: "It's quite tasty."

Kabeer and I were both part of Food from the 'Hood, although I joined later when I entered high school. We both got to know Melinda well, and still to this day see her as a mentor and good friend. At the time, however, Melinda introduced us to concepts and ideas that we otherwise never would have experienced. My parents were living examples of entrepreneurship, but I never learned from them how they did it. Theirs was the sort of gritty entrepreneurship that allowed one to make a living in an uncertain and chaotic world. They got by on their determination, hard work, and independence. These are all important lessons, and I'm thankful to have my parents embody them for me. Melinda taught me a different side of entrepreneurship, the nuts and bolts. The financials. The budgets. The invoices. I never knew how to use a computer until I met Melinda, who made a deal with Apple to donate Macs to Food from the 'Hood. The first time I logged into AOL—"you've got mail"—was with Melinda. The year was 1996, and the Internet was only about a year old—at least as far as the public was concerned. Melinda saw the potential immediately, and perhaps for the first time in the history of Crenshaw High School, some of its students were more technologically advanced than the average American teenager.

My parents never taught us this side of business. It's not the glamorous side, but it's the side that allows one not just to create something for oneself, but *grow it.* We didn't just learn how to start a business, we learned how to run it, how to expand, how to market, how to scale, and how to innovate. Melinda also taught me how money *worked.* My parents might have taught us the value of a dollar and the importance of saving, but we never learned about how money can make money. When I left for San Diego State, it was Melinda who advised me on how to invest my scholarship money. Investing was a completely foreign concept to me. I wasn't going to waste that money—my parents had taught me that much—but to use my money to make *more money?* This was magical stuff, and far beyond what we were learning at Crenshaw.

The seed was planted: We may have been surrounded by devastation, but we could still learn how to create something that was uniquely our own. There was hope. Our situation didn't dictate who we were or what we could be. That was the gift that Melinda gave me, and all us kids who were part of Food from the 'Hood. She showed that this larger, exciting world out there was available to us. What we saw every day—the desolation from the riots, the hopelessness of those who wandered our streets, the tyranny of the gangs and drugs—didn't have to define our world. We could break out.

By giving us a reprieve from our own paralyzing self-doubt, mentors show us new ways of looking at old problems. They help us break free of the prison we too often create in our minds. And if we listen to what they're saying, then suddenly we see the doom we imagined wasn't true after all. The road ahead suddenly doesn't look so dark.

A WORLD OF MENTORS

As human beings, we hunger for companionship and we yearn for guidance. Yet we also tremble at the thought of revealing our true selves to others. What will they think? Will they laugh? Will they walk away?

If you think others would respond this way, then ask yourself this: Would you walk away if someone asked for help? Would you laugh at their need?

You can't expect anyone to help you if you don't ask them. I'm shameless when it comes to talking to strangers. I don't get shy or nervous about introducing myself. It's easy for me to talk to anyone. Some people are shy. But even if I was more or less born with this skill, I also honed it in Food from the 'Hood, when we would travel to expos to meet new clients. We had to learn to be fearless in approaching strangers and making our sales pitch. I have carried this skill with me ever since. I remember when I was at SDSU and I saw the university president walking across the campus. I sprinted to catch up to him and introduce myself. We had a great conversation, but when I returned to the locker room, my teammates were awestruck. "Did you just talk to the president?" they asked, as if it was the most courageous thing someone had ever done. But to me, it was a moment of opportunity. There he was—why wouldn't I talk to him?

But you might be different. If the thought of approaching a potential mentor terrifies you, then try some of these tactics:

★ Go beyond your job or title: When I meet someone for the first time, I talk about my love of travel and that I've been to forty countries. This immediately gets us talking about our shared interests and acts as a great icebreaker.

★ Ask questions: Have an active conversation. Do some homework about your potential mentor and ask relevant questions that engage them and enlighten you.

★ Show a little vulnerability: Once you've established a rapport with someone, you should let them know what you need help with. Tell them where you're struggling and ask what they think you should do.

As one of seven siblings, I learned that closed mouths don't get fed. Open your mouth. Talk. Ask. I guarantee someone will reach out their hand.

We are honored when others seek our guidance and counsel. We are drawn to those who ask for our help. For the same reason we play harder as athletes when we play for our teammates, we need to build a team around us in life. We will play harder when someone is giving us their time. We will play harder when we are helping another. To be mentored and to mentor is to fight for one another.

Why did Sandy Frazier, Mr. Garrison, and Melinda McMullen help a guy like me? Someone who couldn't give them anything in return? Because mentorship is growing another person so that you can grow as a person too.

TO HELP SOMEONE ACHIEVE THEIR DREAMS

I have known Bruce Tollner since I was at San Diego State University. His father, Ted Tollner, was my head coach, and Bruce became the agent representing my brother Kabeer before the 2000 NFL Draft. Selecting an agent was a big decision for my brother, who had a lot of top agencies after him. Bruce wasn't a top agent, at least not at the time. He was just starting out in the industry and hadn't yet made a name for himself. But my brother saw something in Bruce that I would come to see: Bruce Tollner is so much more than a sports agent.

I spent some time with Bruce to talk about the years we have known each other, and we started where our relationship began.

"I had been representing players who were undrafted free agents, but at that point, I had never represented someone who was drafted in the NFL," he says. "I had a home office and I was competing against quality, legitimate agents to represent Kabeer. He saw my passion for representing players and for conducting myself and my business with character and integrity. He believed in me and selected me. That was a special moment."

We stayed in contact, although NCAA rules forced us to keep it strictly personal. I saw how Bruce managed Kabeer's career, and I heard about it directly from my brother. There was something special in the way Bruce treated Kabeer, something that told me Bruce wasn't just another agent.

"I have always strongly believed in treating all people with respect, and I carried this philosophy with me when I started my business of representing football players," Bruce tells me. "Regardless of a person's background or position in life, whether it be football or any other profession, my approach is to treat them with equal reverence. My personal goal is to help my players develop to their fullest potential."

I always knew I wanted Bruce to represent me when—and if—my turn came to go pro. I saw none of the shady, impersonal dealings that college athletes are warned about. My whole life, even to this day, I've had a somewhat paranoid view of my financial affairs. I wanted to know exactly where my money was and what it was doing. (My wife would happily verify this.) Growing up in the hood, I developed a sixth sense for shysters. I call it my hood intuition. There are those agents who try to sign players by selling them on the "big life" in the NFL, all the fame and fortune that awaits them.

Bruce never tried to sell me a pipe dream. From the first moment, he kept it real with me. Even still, I entered the draft feeling nothing but confident. Bruce would take care of me, I knew. Then draft day rolled around and catastrophe struck. I went undrafted. I knew it was possible, but it still came as a shock. I was broken. Although the day would end with the Oakland Raiders inviting me to their training camp as an undrafted free agent, I wondered how this might affect my relationship with Bruce. Undrafted guys just don't bring in the same bucks to an agent that a drafted player does.

I shouldn't have worried.

"It doesn't matter what draft pick or round a player is drafted in; they deserve everything I have to help them go after their dream of playing in the NFL," says Bruce. "I consider myself successful if my commitment as an agent and a friend to each client leads to this result: they look back and believe I helped maximize their opportunities and I had a positive effect on their growth as players and as human beings."

During the tough years, when I bounced around the league from team to team, Bruce was hitting the phones, selling my abilities as if I were Reggie White. Now I know why. For Bruce, my success was his success. But as much as Bruce helped me as an agent, he's had a more profound effect on me as a mentor and dear friend. During major life decisions, Bruce has been there. When I bought my first house, I called Bruce for advice. When I was newly married, I called Bruce.

Hearing Bruce explain it now, I realize that he didn't consider his "job" to be one with boundaries. For him, being an agent was like being a mentor. There was the day-to-day business of negotiating contracts, finding me another team to play for, and making sure that I was taken care of. But the other chosen part of his job had to do with helping me grow as a player and as a person.

"There are so many ups and downs in the agent business and I have been fortunate enough to be around some amazing people and amazing moments," says Bruce. "Every experience where I have been a part of a young man reaching his dream as a top draft pick or even just getting an opportunity to go to a tryout can be special. It is very fulfilling to see somebody work for so long and then be able to reach their dream and set new dreams and goals to go after."

A recurring theme throughout this book is that we don't need to be the greatest to achieve our dreams. I never became the greatest defensive end, but I accomplished my goal of having a career in the NFL because Bruce, my agent, my mentor, fought for me every step of the way.

And when I wanted to charge off into broadcasting, Bruce, who had no financial incentive in my career anymore, helped me plot my course.

"Even though you were released from the team, it wasn't from lack of effort or attitude to be great," he says now. "I was able to witness you take that same incredible, passionate attitude and effort and carry that over to your second career. You are excelling in your second career because of your passion and drive to continue learning and better yourself to be the best you are capable of."

Typical Bruce; he is being too humble. A decade after I retired from the NFL, I became critically ill. Bruce, who lived in Orange County, California, drove to my vacation home in San Diego in the middle of the night to make sure my kids were okay while I stayed in the hospital. That's not something an agent does, particularly for a former client, but it's something Bruce Tollner did.

"To me, investing in a player means that I'm there for them unconditionally, through the highs and lows, and helping them succeed while they are playing and after they leave their last game," Bruce tells me. "The transition from the NFL to a second career can be very challenging. Beyond being their agent, I am also their friend and I want to help any way I can."

Mentors become so because they themselves were once mentored. They understand the impact their attention, advice, and friendship can have on those who ask them for help. And now they want to pass it on. So it was for Bruce, when I asked him about the impact of mentors in his own life. He replied:

"I truly believe it requires multiple people, men and women, to contribute as examples and in mentoring and shaping another person. I was blessed with several great people who have positively impacted me. I am grateful to have learned from others' wisdom, successes, failures, and challenges. Each one of them has been a mentor in different ways and each one of them has had an incredible influence on my life. I find it personally enriching to become involved in someone's life, beyond a business level or social level. Really, truly become involved, pay it forward, and help one another. I believe in the African proverb that says 'It takes a village to raise a child.'"

4

THAT STRENGTH TO
CARRY US THROUGH

During my senior year in high school, I accepted a scholarship from San Diego State University to play football. I chose SDSU for a few reasons. When I was a junior, I had visited Kabeer on campus and met some of his teammates. (And, as a matter of fact, my younger brother, Abdul, would join me at SDSU a couple of years later.) I wanted to be close to home (always a California kid) and I wanted to see how my brother had navigated football and academics. I was redshirted my freshman year, which means that I was on the team, but not allowed to play in a game. Teams redshirt freshmen to give them an extra year of eligibility, because the game changes so drastically between high school and college. To be redshirted says something about the team's expectations of you. They want to give you a buffer year to better understand the game and learn the team's system.

And, yes, I needed all the buffer time I could get. I had left high school with an *appreciation* for the game of football, but not a deep understanding. I did what the coaches had told me to do, and I had done it well enough to catch the attention of scouts. But I still had a lot to learn. I remember early in my college career Coach Ken Delgado getting so frustrated with my ignorance of the game. During one practice, when he told me to line up in front of a specific offensive lineman, I hesitated. I didn't know the positions on the offensive line. That did it.

He grabbed me and took me down the offensive line. "This is the center!" he shouted, pointing to the guy who snaps the ball. "This is the guard!" Pointing to the guy who's next to the center. "This is the tackle!" The next guy down the line. "And this is the tight end!" Coach Delgado used more colorful language, but you get the point. He was angry and I was embarrassed, as I should have been.

I made it to San Diego State on a full-ride scholarship, but not without strings. Even though I was a redshirt freshman, I still needed to graduate in four years for a chance to be eligible for a fifth year. That put a lot of pressure on me to do well not only on the field but also in the classroom. I felt like I was working against a timer. I had seen some action my second year on the squad against Hawaii and San Jose State, but it wasn't until my third year that I started working into the rotation. I finished the season with fourteen tackles, including a sack in the final game of the year against Wyoming. I also had the joy of starting alongside my brother for several games. When I started my fourth year, time was running short to make an impact.

On August 31, 2000, San Diego State played Arizona State in the first game of the season. Before the game, I could feel my heart pounding through my pads—way more than usual, that is. Everyone's pumped for opening day, especially when you're playing in front of the home crowd at Qualcomm Stadium. But this opening day was special for me. I saw it as my coming-out party. In fact, I saw the whole upcoming season as the one where the football world would take notice of me.

Kabeer had been drafted by the Packers, and I was now an every-game starter. I had two seasons left to prove myself. Two seasons to show the world that the other Gbajabiamila could play too. I had finally laid my basketball dreams to rest. I was a football player. I had spent the off-season doing almost nothing except studying football and working on my game. This game against ASU was where it would all start. And I didn't shrink from the pressure. Even though we lost, I roared like a lion that day, with seven tackles (already half of my 1999 total), including a sack. I was also up against one of the toughest left tackles in college, Levi Jones, who would go on to play eight seasons in the NFL.

After that game I was on top of the world. I had done what I had set out to do: put my mark on the team and prove that I belonged. I was on my way. An NFL scout would tell me a little later that if I played like I did against ASU all the time, I would be a shoo-in for the draft.

The day after the game, we gathered as a team to break down the film and the coaches praised my performance. After the film I hopped on my bike to ride home, as happy as I had ever been as a football player. I *was* a football player. It had taken years for me to get to this point, but now it was all coming together. The next game was against Illinois, Big Ten territory. Man, I knew I could dominate and show that ASU was no fluke. Akbar Gbajabiamila had arrived.

Then, catastrophe. During my ride home, my tire blew out and I ran into the curb. The pedal came down on my left leg and I felt a pop in my calf as I hit the cement. This was a bit disconcerting. I'm left-legged (and left-handed), which means that I get all my explosive speed and power by pushing off from my left. Hobbling into the locker room, the team trainers thought I had just bruised my muscle; nothing a couple of shots of painkillers couldn't handle. What a relief! On to the Fighting Illini. But by Saturday, game day, neither my limp nor the pain was any better. I saw a doctor that day, who started poking around my calf. He diagnosed me in minutes.

"You've torn your Achilles tendon," he said.

I let the words slowly sink into my head. I heard what he said; I knew what it meant; but I had to ask anyway.

"When can I play again?"

The doctor thought a moment before replying, "You'll be out twelve to sixteen months."

Twelve to sixteen months. My season, my coming-out season, was over. It also meant that next season, my last season, was almost certainly shot too.

I started to cry, then I started to get mad. They had to call in the coach to stop me from throwing things in the training room, but I didn't care.

It was over. I was done. Finished.

"YOU'RE COMING OVER TO THIS SIDE"

Injuries are a part of my story. During every major phase of my athletic career, I experienced an injury severe enough to require surgery. In high school, I had made the junior varsity basketball team as a sophomore, which is impressive enough when you're talking about a powerhouse like Crenshaw. But my heart—and all my energy—was set on making the varsity team. My junior year was the year it was all going to happen, but I still had a long way to go. At six feet two, I was a big guy, certainly tall enough to dunk, only I couldn't. It was embarrassing. Before practice, the guys would play around in the gym, and there was almost always a mini dunk contest. Now, dunking like Michael Jordan doesn't make you a great basketball player; but for me, who couldn't join in on the prepractice dunk contest, it made me painfully aware of how far behind I was as a player.

I had another problem, however. My left knee had been giving me a lot of problems during my sophomore year. I would eventually learn that I had suffered cartilage damage, but at the time I didn't know what was going on. The only thing I knew was that after a game or practice, my left knee would swell to the size of a grapefruit. We didn't have any medical insurance growing up. That meant I never saw a doctor. I didn't even have a dentist as a child. Our family just couldn't afford one.

I tried using a knee sleeve but, unbeknownst to me, I was allergic to the neoprene. I would break out in rashes, with huge lumps all around my knee. At times, the reaction got so bad that little pustules would form on my skin. My father would wrap an Ace bandage around the knee to shield it from the sleeve, but I still broke out.

Finally, one of the coaches had me go see a doctor who worked with the Los Angeles Dodgers. He discovered the damage and I got orthoscopic surgery in the summer before my junior year, 1996. Not only did the procedure cost my parents a fortune, but I was devastated. In college and the NFL, every surgery is followed by an intensive rehabilitation regimen, overseen by trainers and doctors. I had none of that. My "rehab" was my healing period, sitting on my butt, which was going to take up the entire summer—the very summer I had planned to focus on practice and getting ready for the varsity team. Now it looked like that dream was over.

With nothing else to do, I had time to reflect, and it proved more valuable than had I gone with my original plan. I was able to stop, sit, and realize where I was. My dream of making the varsity team, and beyond that, playing ball in college, was in serious jeopardy. I had to admit that time was running out on me. I developed a sense of urgency that drove me to reconsider the way I practiced, worked out, and prepared to play. When I finally was able to move around a little, I started training again. I had developed a fresh determination to make the varsity team. I would train not only harder, but smarter. And that's where my personal coach and mentor, Sandy Frazier, helped me most. He taught me to see my defects, the parts of my game that were nowhere near the level they needed to be. It wasn't just dunking; I couldn't dribble, and I needed help on my fundamentals. He also served as my rehab specialist and trainer. The people at the rehab center treated me like just another patient: a kid like any other kid. But Sandy understood that I would never get to the level I needed to be at if I followed the traditional rehab schedule. He helped accelerate my healing so that I could get back to training faster.

The summer ended, and the season began. I started on the JV squad, but something had changed. I was a different player, a better player. While the other guys could tell I was better, I had kept something back from them. Then, during one of those prepractice dunk contests, I got on the court and slammed a few home. Yes, it was finally showtime. A six-feet-two (going quickly on six feet three) player who could dunk, thanks to Sandy Frazier.

The coaches took notice too. One day the legendary varsity coach Willie West walked into the JV gym and pointed at me. "Akbar," he shouted, "you're coming over to this side." I couldn't run fast enough. The varsity team needed me to play against Oak Hill Academy, one of the top programs on the East Coast. That Oak Hill team was stacked, boasting on Stephen Jackson, who would go on to become one of the greats in the NBA. The game was to be played at the University of California, Irvine campus, for the Nike Extravaganza, which brought together the best teams from around the country. Crenshaw needed a power forward and I fit the bill, having learned to emulate the great power forwards of the time—Charles Barkley and Dennis Rodman.

I know that without the surgery I wouldn't have had the sense of urgency. Had I continued to do what I had been doing, I wouldn't have made the gains. The injury and surgery had allowed me to get away from everything for a bit. To stop. To think. To start over. The injury gave me the time I needed to figure out my priorities—what did I really want and how could I achieve that? While I had thought that being hobbled with the knee was the moment my dream slipped away into "never," in fact, it was exactly what I needed. That, and Mr. Frazier's help.

We view setbacks, like injuries, as impediments along our journey. Sometimes it's very hard to see the positive when you're sitting on your couch, letting the days roll by without getting any closer to your goal. But I discovered that we can use those moments to prioritize. Every moment can be used to push you further toward your goal, even if it's used solely for reflection.

THE DARK VALLEY

My knee would flare up over the next several years, as I shifted my focus from basketball to football. I would need surgery again in 1998, while at San Diego State, which shut me down for spring ball. And then another one in 1999.

But nothing quite prepared me for my Achilles tendon injury in 2000. I was staring at more than a year away from the game, a year that I couldn't afford to lose. As I mentioned, my clock for making an impact was running out. The year 2001 was going to be my last year, and it looked like I would miss most, if not all, of it. Teams can't afford to wait around for a player to come back, especially not for those who haven't quite shown their worth yet.

A couple of months after the accident, I was quoted in the campus newspaper, *The Daily Aztec*, for a story about my injury and what it meant for the team. "The injury is so frustrating," I had said. "I'm almost thinking of retirement. It's so frustrating to go out to practice and games and not be able to do anything. I can't wait to get back on the field and play."

Internally, I was a mess. I quickly ballooned to three hundred pounds because I was eating to silence the emotional pain. My mind went to dark places too. The ASU game did more for me than show the football world that I belonged. It was also when I first started to think about making the NFL. I had been playing football for only five years, and I never really let myself imagine that the NFL was a possibility. But that ASU game had given me the confidence that I did belong. That I could be great at this sport. My dream to play in the NFL started after that ASU game.

And just like that, it was snatched away from me. What kind of cruelty is that? I went from being a monster on the field to being wheeled out of the hospital. I went from the best physical shape of my life to having my roommate help me take a shower.

So when I talked about "retirement" in that interview, I was being serious. I had fallen back on schoolwork as my one remaining salvation. I felt like if I couldn't succeed academically, I would find myself back home, working as a grocery clerk or something.

"Hey, Akbar, whatever happened to you, man?"

"Paper or plastic?"

I plunged myself into my schoolwork so that I didn't have to think about the pain of the sideline. Athletes know what I'm talking about, but the worst place a player can be is on the sideline watching. You certainly miss the playing, but you know what you miss more? The team and your friends. The sharing of victory, struggle, and defeat. I was still on the team, but I wasn't a part of the team anymore. Or at least that's how I felt. And it wasn't like I just sprained my ankle. I had an injury that ruined careers. Some people never come back from an Achilles tendon injury. Even if I did get back to my old form, I would likely be out of college by then. Either way, my playing days were probably over. How could I just sit on the sideline watching?

It was at this moment, while I was rehabbing and going through some of my darkest valleys, that my mother came to me. My mother never cared about my athletic career. She hadn't even come to see me play at SDSU. But the moment her baby was hurt, she came down to help. I remember her sitting beside me, my leg in a cast, and saying, "We're going to pray." And so, we prayed.

"You'll be healed in the name of God," she said. My mother, like all Nigerians, didn't just use her words to speak. She used her whole body. And would say again and again, eyes wide with passion: "Any doctor who says you can't come back, I cast that into the sea!" Her arms would shoot out into the air, as if she were really casting something far out into the distant ocean.

I dared to express my doubts.

"Do you believe?" she retorted, in her thick Nigerian accent.

"But Mama . . ."

"Do you believe?"

I had been raised in a dual-religion household. My father was a Muslim, my mother a devout Christian. That might seem odd to those who haven't experienced such an upbringing, but to us kids it was normal. We prayed in both religions and I never saw this as a problem when I was a child. Of course, that changed when I grew up and went to San Diego. Most of the guys in the locker room were Christian, but there were other Muslims, like Ephraim Salaam and Az-Zahir Hakim, both of whom would go on to have prominent NFL careers. I felt like I was a Muslim at this time because I identified more with my father as head of the household. That's what he was and that's what I would be. Then I went through my "no religion" phase. I think most people go through a period like this in their life, when they start to question the assumptions and truths they believed as a child. I never gave up on God, but I didn't identify with any religion.

This went on for about a year and a half. In 1999, the pastor Miles McPherson of Rock Church started preaching at San Diego State and immediately created a buzz on campus. I went to go hear him speak. McPherson, a former NFL player and recovering drug addict, mesmerized me in a way that I had never experienced before. He wasn't a screamer or "fire-and-brimstone" preacher. He was a teacher. He taught me the word of God. He preached about his own troubles and how one must rely on scripture to find the way forward. For someone who had never been taught religion—I was "raised" religiously—I took to McPherson like a student to a teacher. That year, because of McPherson, I decided to give my life to Christ.

"Do you believe?"

Yes, Mama, I believe.

With my mother's help, I slowly began to realize that I could only get stronger by trusting in the Lord with all my heart. The hard work would come, but at that moment, I had to put my faith in Him. If I was supposed to be a football player, then He would give me the strength to be one. If I wasn't, then He would show me other paths.

Those moments with my mother provided me with another gift. My brothers and sister had always teased me that I had been Mama's favorite. Maybe I was, but I always had empathy for her. Despite her alcoholism, I was able to give her grace. It's no disrespect to say that she was a ferocious woman; temperamental and passionate. Whatever she did, she did with everything she had. This sometimes created problems while I was growing up, both for us kids and for my father, but during my recovery, when she would come down to see me, I really saw her. With her by my bedside and in the weeks that followed, I formed a relationship with her that made us closer. Yet sitting with her, as she would utter prayers and rub special oils on my calf, we talked about a lot, including things like sex, which we had *never* talked about before.

She also told me a story about when my oldest brother, Foley, was born. She was already in the States, pregnant, when her mother back in Nigeria passed. But no one told her. They feared that the pain might cause her to lose the baby. As she told me this story, she started to cry. She hadn't shared a lot of her stories about Nigeria, or the family she left. I had only known what was in front of me. I realized then that I didn't know my mother at all. And something happened: I started to see her in a different light. I could see her inner strength and I could see a woman who believed in God with every fiber of her being. I used to dismiss her wild exclamations, but now I saw that they came from a deep well of love for God.

"May God go before you, go behind you, and go with you," she would say. Now I finally understood what she meant.

About four or five months into my recovery, I visited the trainer for a check-in. He poked and prodded and had me move around as much as I could on crutches. I asked him how much more time I needed. His reply: "About another year." That should have sealed my fate. Wiser men accept reality, because living in a fantasy world only delays the inevitable heartbreak. But something changed in me then. I didn't accept his answer. You could say I refused his prognosis.

"Just watch," I said to Gary Johnson, the head athletic trainer. "I'm going to be a medical miracle." We shared a laugh, but what he didn't realize was that I had meant it. I was done feeling sorry for myself. I was done sulking and imagining my life in a grocery store. I had not come so far to have it snatched away from me just at my moment to shine. That wasn't how it was supposed to go.

Through God—and my mother—I had rediscovered my determination. I started to *believe* I would get better.

I began to grow increasingly frustrated with my rehab schedule. The daily routine of icing and ultrasounds started to feel like I was treading water. My trainers' daily reminder to "just be patient" quickly became like nails on a chalkboard. I didn't have time to be patient! I had to take control. What I needed was to just get moving again. I was six months into my recovery and only a couple of months away from spring ball. But I also didn't want my coaches to think I was endangering my recovery with careless activity—even though I kind of was. So I started to jog around the track, which is above a parking garage and looks down on the football field. I thought I was safe from prying eyes, because those on the field can't see who's on the track.

Even then, I got caught. Johnson saw me running one day and asked what in the world I was doing.

"I'm rehabbing," I said. He just shook his head. And he probably had every reason to do so. I wasn't supposed to be pushing the fragile tendon like that, and, truthfully, I was scared to death of reinjuring it. But I had no other choice. If I couldn't make it back in time for the season, I was done. If I reinjured my tendon, I was done. So I might as well risk a reinjury.

My tenacity did cause Johnson to accelerate my rehab schedule, pushing me harder than he would have otherwise. But I knew I could do more. I had that gut instinct that told me I could. It's hard to tell an expert that they're wrong, and I never really said that to Johnson. Instead, I sort of made my determination to come back a running joke with him. I started calling my tendon my "bionic Achilles." I would tease him with ridiculous statements like, "Who's the guy who's going to be a medical marvel?" or "They're going to write in medical journals about me!"

I was kidding, but only just. My thoughts had begun to change. I started preaching positive affirmations to myself, not just in front of Johnson. I would find inspiration from the great sports comeback stories, like Michael Jordan's "flu game" or Magic Johnson's "comeback game" in 1996 (a game my friends and I snuck into, just so I could see Magic coming out of the tunnel), after being away from the sport for five years. Magic got nineteen points, ten assists, and eight rebounds that game—nearly a triple-double. I started having glorious visions of my triumphant return. The sports pages would be filled with headlines like, "The Greatest Comeback Ever!" Talk about being an underdog, I was going to show the whole world that Akbar Gbajabiamila wasn't done. The world hadn't seen everything there was to see yet.

I kept up the pace, running farther and faster each week. The months ticked by. Seven months. Eight months. Spring had come around and the team was gearing up for spring camp. At the last practice of spring ball, I "took off the restraints," so to speak, and went full bore. Exploding off the starting line. The medical miracle was happening.

It was now May, nine months since the injury, six months away from when I was supposed to be "healed." But I was back. I had defied all the odds and the opinions of medical professionals.

I was back on the team. I was moved to defensive tackle, because I had put on fifty pounds, but I was still playing ball again. The miracle was complete.

When I look at that experience today, I see the power of my determination. I rejected what the brightest guys in the room said about me. That doesn't happen to everyone. Sometimes, the brightest guys in the room are right. But had I listened to them, I wouldn't have made it to the NFL. I wouldn't be writing this book today. I would have allowed outside forces to influence what I knew to be true in my heart: that I wasn't supposed to go out like that.

But I also think about those dark days, when I wallowed in my own misery. I think about how I let myself be nearly consumed by my own pity. I used to be ashamed at that, but I have a different view today. Now I believe that it was good for my eventual recovery to go through that dark valley. I had to let my mind grapple with the tragic news; it needed to go dark before I could see the light again.

And what I learned from the experience is that I was able to take control of my own destiny when others said I couldn't. I speak mostly of the medical professionals here, but I want to make it clear that I don't blame them. Nor am I saying that we should ignore what experts tell us. But it strikes me that now I put my faith in my own recovery in the only two things that mattered: God and myself. God gave me the strength to rediscover my determination and passion to excel. But it was up to me to do something with that. God wasn't going to heal me with me just sitting on my butt. I had to take the strength He had given me and do something with it.

God designed us all for His purpose. We're given talents and gifts to grow His kingdom. Without that kind of power in your life, it's hard to accomplish anything. But it's nearly impossible during moments of incredible pain and doubt. When we find ourselves in one of those moments, when our dream looks like it's come to an end, that's when we need to find the courage to believe that we are going through the dark valley for a reason. I wouldn't have been the player that I ended up being if not for my Achilles tendon injury. But more important, I wouldn't be the man I am without that injury.

Fans of *American Ninja Warrior* often ask me if the excitement and craziness I display during the show is real. Or, as some suspect, am I just putting on an act? It's real. It's real because I know that those competitors often went through their own dark valley to get to that course. I cheer like crazy for the ninjas because I have walked through the valleys. I made it through and they made it through. Who wouldn't cheer like a freaking madman for that?

As it happened, I ended up getting an extra year of eligibility. The year 2001 wouldn't be my last season after all. Time to move on.

Oh, and my mother started to come to all my games.

MY GREATEST INJURY

Up till now, you might think that the worst injury I sustained as a player was snapping my Achilles tendon. That was indeed a transformational moment for me, one that changed the way I looked at not only athletics but at life. Yet it pales in comparison to the injury I suffered six days before my last college football game. The scars from that injury have never healed.

The last game of the season was against the University of Hawaii in Honolulu. I was having the best season of my college career and had been named to the All–Mountain West team. Things couldn't have been going better. I had received an additional year of eligibility and had my sights firmly set on the NFL Draft just a few short months ahead. The pain and memory of my Achilles tendon accident were in the past; I had moved on, stronger, faster, and more mature in my outlook on what I needed to do to get to the next level. Kabeer was in the NFL by this point, crushing quarterbacks and running backs for the Green Bay Packers and making a name for himself throughout the league. Although I had stopped trying to emulate his playing style, I still saw him as an example of how far I could go, if I worked hard enough.

At 4–8, it had been a disappointing season for SDSU, but we were coming off a close 38–34 win over Air Force and wanted to end the season on a high note. I, as well as the rest of the seniors, particularly those who knew this would be their last college football game ever, wanted to finish the season strong. I had one last chance to show the NFL scouts that another Gbajabiamila deserved a spot in the league.

Then, six days before the game, on December 1, 2002, I got the news that my mother had been killed in a car accident. I was in my apartment when my phone rang. It was my sister, Kubrat, who was frantic. What a difference a few hours makes. Earlier that day, we had all received news that Kabeer was going to be a father. In fact, my brother Abdul, who also lived in San Diego, had been at the house in LA when they had heard from Kabeer and had driven down to San Diego that evening.

"Mama hit someone!" That was about all I could get out of Kubrat. I called my dad, but he didn't pick up. My sister called back and told me that our mother was dead. Abdul and I drove home to LA. I started to have a panic attack on the interstate and slammed my hand so hard against the steering wheel that I bent it. Abdul, who always had a knack for calming me down, had me pull off to the side of the road so I could collect myself. It was a long drive, but we made it home. I saw the scene of the accident, which was only a few blocks down the road from our house. She had slammed into one of the tall palm trees that lined the road (on the other side of the road), flipping the car, which came to a stop in front of a neighbor's house. I also saw my father, who was trying to remain calm and be the rock he had always been, and I called my coach. He told me to take all the time I needed and that he would break the news to the team. I stayed in LA for three more days to be with the family. The funeral wasn't going to happen until the following week, but I had two decisions to make. Should I go back to school? And should I travel with the team to Hawaii?

I decided to go back to school, if only to get away from everything. I still wasn't sure if I was going to Hawaii, but I didn't practice. I wasn't sure what to do, but Coach Delgado gave me some advice. "I don't think you want to go back and see your mom like that," he said. "It'll be the last image you have of her." I listened, trying to keep it together, but I heeded his advice. I didn't go back home. I stayed at school, and two days later we left for Hawaii. I broke down on the plane, like the wall I had erected between my brain and my emotions just collapsed, unleashing a torrent of tears and anguish.

When we landed I didn't know what I was going to do. Of course, the coaches and my teammates would understand if I didn't play. How could I, in the state I was in?

I started to remember moments from my childhood, when my mother and father would be fighting, and things would get really heated. I would leave the house and go to the basketball court, just to get my mind off things. It was cathartic. As an athlete, you learn to compartmentalize your emotions. You're never going to enter game day in a perfect mental state. There's always something to distract you and take your focus off the game. The greatest players can focus like it's a superpower, but even the average ones learn this skill. We learn to deal with the pain by focusing on something else. That's what I did as a child to escape the house, and that's what I had done as an athlete.

I also remembered what my father would tell me, the very thing he told me when I wanted to quit football. "You started something, you finish it." I decided to play. I had started this journey and I would finish it. I didn't play *for my mom* so much as I did to escape the pain. Playing itself was one of those out-of-body experiences. Years later I was knocked out during a game against the Cowboys and I remember lying on the field, looking up at the ceiling but not hearing anything. It was like I was the only one in the stadium.

That's how my last college football game felt to me. I was the only one there. I had never been more focused, more driven to complete my task. And I played like a lion that day. After the game, I let the focus go, and the pain hit me again. My task had been completed.

When we are sidelined by injury, physical or mental, we miss something if we don't use those moments to our greatest advantage. When we are on a path toward our dreams, every moment stands as an opportunity to put us closer to achievement or keep us where we are. We often view injuries in a negative light, which is entirely understandable. They keep us from being in the game. All else being equal, we would rather *not* get hurt. But we can't control everything that happens to us. And injuries will happen. Pain, physical or mental, will hit you at the worst possible moment. You won't always be at your best.

And then there are those moments when you must play through the pain, when you must fall back on everything that got you to that point and believe it will carry you forward. I'm talking about training, mental preparation, practice, and all the little things that we do so we can perform at our best, even when we're not at our best. But I'm also talking about relying on the strength and love of something greater than yourself. For me, that's God. I don't turn to God only during times of pain. I keep my relationship with Him strong during the good times *so* that when I enter those valleys, my faith remains strong and resilient. *So* that I don't wonder why fate has been so cruel and allow myself to wallow in self-pity. I know He will get me through.

The habits you form during the good times are the ones that will get you through the bad times.

"I'VE NEVER SEEN ANYTHING LIKE THIS"

There was a moment early in Zach Gowen's run during the 2016 Indianapolis qualifying round that I realized I was watching something that defied explanation. By this point in my hosting duties for *American Ninja Warrior*, I had seen a lot. I had witnessed the sick and the disadvantaged accomplish the impossible. But I'd never seen anything like Zach Gowen, and I said as much on air. Neither had anyone else. On the sidelines that night, Kacy Catanzaro was in tears.

When Zach was eight years old, a soccer ball shot directly at Zach's left leg had shattered the bone, an odd result from a child kicking a ball. Over the next several months, Zach's leg kept breaking because of trivial injuries, and the doctors were baffled. Then they found out why. Zach had a malignant tumor on his femur, and it was almost too late. Zach spent the next several months at the children's hospital in Detroit, fighting for his life.

"I lost my leg to the battle of cancer, but I won the war of life," is how Zach describes it.

Sadly, losing his leg wouldn't be the only tragedy to befall Zach in his childhood. When Zach was just four, his father, who suffered from substance abuse, left the family. It isn't any wonder that for most of his young life, Zach felt "ugly, defective, and not good enough." But Zach found an outlet for his frustrations and a source of joy: professional wrestling.

"When I watched wrestling, all my feelings of not having my leg, of being sick, and being without a dad just went away," he told me. "At sixteen, it was the only thing I was passionate about. I told everybody I was going to be a professional wrestler. And everyone just patronized me. What's funny is that I didn't think having one leg was going to be much of a problem. My small size was going to be a problem."

As it turned out, neither Zach's missing leg nor his small size stopped him from becoming a professional wrestler before he was twenty-one. He started training at a small wrestling school in his hometown in Michigan. He wore long pants on his first day to hide his prosthetic leg. When it was his turn to get into the ring, he tore off his pants to reveal his "handicap." He kept his head down to avoid the reaction of the other students, but to Zach's joy, the trainer, Brian Shotwell, just looked at him and asked, "You wrestled in high school?" Zach nodded. "Good," he said, "all my best students wrestled in high school."

That was it. Zach got in the ring. By treating him like everyone else, Brian gave Zach the bit of confidence boost he needed to forget what made him different, and to just do what he loved. Not only did he love it, but Zach was very good at it. In January 2003, he signed with WWE. Despite the odds, everything was coming together for Zach Gowen.

He was fired six months later.

"I was emotionally immature and not ready to receive that gift," says Zach. "I didn't take it seriously. I was a kid having fun, and I had a bad attitude and trouble with commitment." WWE had had enough.

But there was something else going on in the background, something that would come to consume Zach's life—and nearly destroy it. He had always loved having a good time—booze, drugs, and women. When he lost his job, he suddenly lost his identity. The fans, the money, and the women were all gone. The two things that remained were the drugs and the booze, and Zach embraced them like a drowning man on a life raft.

"I was passionate about my pursuit of getting high," he says today. "But the solution to my problem became my problem." In other words, drugs and alcohol had helped Zach get through tough moments in his life, by dulling the pain and offering an escape. But they stopped doing either, instead trapping Zach in a vicious cycle of substance abuse that threatened to destroy his life.

Zach recalls a moment when he was living in Detroit delivering pizzas, spending his days drunk, high, or trying to get drunk or high. He was on a delivery one night when he was robbed at gunpoint. The robber took Zach's car and money. What the guy didn't get, and what Zach truly cared about, were the two Oxy-Contin pills he had in his sock. He walked home and got high.

"That should've given me sufficient reason to stop," he says. "Normal people would've stopped. But I kept using for two years."

By the time Zach was twenty-six, he was living with his mother. He tried to conceal his addictions from her, but she could usually tell. One day, she found him and asked if he was high. Yes, he said. But then he said something that he hadn't in all those years of struggling with his disease.

"I don't want to be, Mom," he said. "I'm scared, and I need help."

On February 14, 2010, Zach was on a plane to treatment. He's been sober ever since.

"Reaching out to another human being was the genesis of my recovery," he told me. He discovered that WWE had a wellness program open to anyone who had had a contract with the company. They would pay for inpatient treatment and aftercare. "Even though I wasn't making a dime for WWE, they helped me," he says.

Now sober and living his life "by spiritual principles," as he told me, Zach returned to his first passion, wrestling. WWE rehired him. But Zach has also found a second career in speaking with others about his life. He talks about losing his father and his leg as a child, but, surprisingly, these topics aren't what Zach focuses on. He talks about his addiction, his disease, and how every day he tries to be of service to others.

You and I might think this selflessness is incredible, but for Zach, it's a matter of life or death. By helping others—to get sober, get fit, and find their spiritual path—Zach stays alive.

"Everything I do is rooted in me being of service to others," he says. "If I don't, the consequences of my deterioration will be devastating. Either I continue on a spiritual path or I die."

When I spoke to Zach, I figured we'd spend most of our time together talking about his leg. It was only after a few minutes of conversation that I realized that Zach's dark valley wasn't his leg. It wasn't his absentee father either. It was the five years he spent mired in drugs and alcohol.

When Zach stepped onto the *Ninja* course in Indianapolis, I didn't just see an amputee. I saw an amputee remove his prosthesis and literally throw it away. He drew attention to his lost limb by showing the world that it wasn't a problem. We should applaud that. It is inspiring, and I was dumbfounded that Zach made it through two obstacles before falling.

Only now when I see Zach, I don't just see someone who has managed to live a normal, incredibly active life with just one leg. I don't just see someone who can do on one leg what most people can't do on two.

I see a survivor, a man who had to walk through his own dark valley of addiction before he could find his purpose and rediscover his passion for life. The inspiration behind Zach's story isn't only that a one-legged man was standing on the *Ninja* course; it's that a *sober* man was standing there. Zach's real injury wasn't the leg he lost as a child. He learned to overcome that and thrive. No, Zach's real injury was his addiction—the part of him that no one saw, but that nearly destroyed him. How he overcame that—and the man he is today—is a far greater story than an amputee walking up to the *Ninja* course and dramatically tossing his prosthetic leg into the air.

Early in our conversation, Zach expressed a familiar sentiment: "The two most important days in a man's life are the day he was born and the day he finds out why."

Zach's "why" didn't come to him after he lost his leg. "The 'why' came to me after I hit rock bottom. My purpose is to carry my message and share my story."

5

FEAR IS OUR GREATEST ENEMY

The 2003 NFL Draft took place over seven rounds on April 26 and 27. I watched the draft at the family house of my teammate and friend J. R. Tolver, who was selected in the fifth round. My thinking behind watching with J.R. was because we had taken this journey together. We had played together; we would get drafted together; and then we would celebrate together. I had just finished my sixth season at SDSU and was confident that I would be drafted. I knew I wouldn't be picked in the first few rounds, but certainly in the fifth or sixth. The seventh, if I was truly unlucky. Even when J.R. was drafted, and I was still "on the boards," I didn't really worry. I had spoken with my agent, Bruce Tollner, earlier in the day, but otherwise I kept my phone open. You never know when a team might call and the last thing you want is for a potential employer to get a busy signal. So all my friends and family knew to let me be.

Yet as the day drew on and my plan started to fall apart, the rounds ticked by and 262 players were drafted. I had trouble controlling my emotions. I knew Bruce was working the phones furiously, but mine stayed horribly silent.

When the last name of the last round was called, I had tears in my eyes. I ran out of J.R.'s parents' house and found myself on a nearby golf course, crying. Had I expected to be drafted? Absolutely. It wasn't arrogance or an inflated belief in my own abilities either. To understand why I had such confidence, we need to go back a year to the end of my fifth season at SDSU. I had been selected to the All–Mountain West team and been chosen to play in the college All-Star East-West Shrine game. But I had also been awarded a *sixth season* in college because of my Achilles tendon injury. This happens, but it's very rare. I could have entered the 2002 Draft, but after talking about it with Bruce, I decided to come back to school and play out the next season. Before Draft Day in 2002, Bruce even got a call from the Colts, expressing interest in me. He had to tell them I wasn't entering the draft.

There was a risk in going back to school. I could get hurt or I could have a bad year. Either one would jeopardize my chances of getting drafted. Neither happened. I also had a very good friend who was behind me on the depth chart—meaning he would take over my starting position if I left—and I knew how excited he was. But I didn't even consider how my return to SDSU would disrupt his football future. To this day, I regret not giving it any thought. I didn't enter the draft because I thought that I could only help my chances the following year with another season of college experience. I still felt very new to the game, despite the great strides I had taken at San Diego State. And for a while, it seemed like I had made the right decision. In fact, I was chosen for the All-Star East-West Shrine game again and became one of the few players in history to be selected two years in a row (it's only for seniors). At the end of my sixth and final season, I was healthy, I was strong, and I was ready.

While there was that small voice in the back of my mind reminding me that the draft can be unpredictable, I didn't pay it much attention. I learned a valuable lesson (eventually): Just because I *should have been* drafted, it doesn't mean I *would be* drafted. The world doesn't work like a math problem. You can't add this to that and get the same result over and over. There are variables in life, most outside our control, and nothing should be taken for granted.

The sting of not being drafted was bad enough. But what made it even worse was that I felt I had made a mistake going back to college for my sixth season. What if I had been drafted by the Colts? I'd have been part of a great 4–3 defense playing alongside players like Dwight Freeney, who was drafted in the first round in 2002. I also wouldn't have lost one of my best friends from childhood. My friend, who was right behind me in the rotation at SDSU, never forgave me for coming back—and I never forgot.

It's a terrible moment for anyone to think that they might have made a choice that proved to be a mistake. We wonder if that was it: our one shot at greatness, denied because we went left when we should have gone right. When our decisions don't work out—or don't seem to work out on our schedule—then we tend to look backward, not ahead. We see all the work and effort we put in toward achieving our dreams as wasted. If it can all come crashing down because of one decision (that seemed right at the time), then why bother doing all that work again? When I stormed out of my friend's house on Draft Day, I was convinced my career was over. At the time I couldn't see a way back onto the path toward the NFL, my dream. My head was stuck in the past, cursing my luck. My one shot lost!

And that's where we sometimes go astray. We get so focused on the path we are on that it's difficult to see that there are many paths we can take. For me, I was *supposed* to be drafted. That was my path; that was the culmination of everything I had worked toward. There was no other way.

Like anything else, we get comfortable being on the path we're on. It's still hard work, but it's familiar and we can see where it's headed. But when life intervenes, as it did for me on Draft Day, we must embark on a different road, one that is frightening because it's unknown. It's also new. We are fearful of the unknown, but we're also fearful of trying something else. For me, the goal was the same—make the NFL—but the path to get there had suddenly changed.

A GLORIFIED INTERVIEW

On Draft Day, J.R. found me crying on the golf course, and we went back to his house. Then Bruce called. His exact words were: "How about the silver and black?" The Raiders had invited me to camp. I was overjoyed but cautious. The odds were still stacked against me, if only because of who the Raiders had drafted. Two defensive ends (one in the first round and the other in the fourth) and a linebacker (in the third round), who the team hoped to use as an alternate defensive lineman. So really, with a veteran presence at defensive end and a multitude of draft picks chosen to do my job, I had little hope of making the team. When I arrived at camp, they confirmed my fears by giving me number 69 and putting me in the auxiliary locker room, which is where they put the guys no one expects to make it. Yes, I got all the tasteless jokes thrown my way by veterans and rookies alike, but forget all that. Sixty-nine is an offensive lineman's number; it's a number you give to a scrub on the defense. It said something (to me, at least) about the Raiders' expectations.

I should have been afraid. Only I wasn't. I had seen this moment play out in my head for so long that it was almost a reality for me. Yes, I was nervous. I didn't know if I would make the team, and, if I didn't, what I was going to do with my life. But I was on the precipice of achieving everything I had worked toward since I was a child growing up in South Central. I was going to embrace the moment, give it everything I had, and let fate decide.

I also thrive when I'm able to prove myself. Wearing 69, being in the auxiliary locker room, though embarrassing, motivated me.

I had some supporters too—Rod Woodson, for one. The Hall of Fame defensive back, who had been in the league sixteen years already, believed in me—and even stuck his neck out for me. He told the coaches, "If you cut this dude, I'm out of here."

Then the cuts started coming. I survived the first cuts, practiced for another week, then survived the second. But I didn't let myself start to believe quite yet. During the last day of cuts, I knew that if I made it to 1:00 p.m., when the horn blew for practice, I had made the team. You can't imagine the anxiety that grips someone in those moments, watching the clock tick down, staring at it, like you're willing it to move faster. I was so nervous that at one point I hid behind the door of the auxiliary locker room. My thinking was that if they can't see you, they can't cut you. I know, it's ridiculous, but your mind starts doing funny things when your dream is on the line.

I looked at my watch. It said 12:58 p.m. Had I made it? There were still two minutes left. But I wasn't about to be late for practice, so I got out from behind the locker room door and ran out to the field. I passed veteran linebacker Bill Romanowski on my way. Another guy like Woodson who had been in the league more than fifteen years, Romanowski probably got a kick out of seeing rookies like me sweat it out on the last day.

"Hey, congrats, you made it," he called after me. Not yet. There was still a minute left. . . .

Then the horn blew.

After practice, I walked back to the auxiliary locker room, but my stuff wasn't there. "We've moved your stuff," the equipment manager told me. I was in the real locker room, with the team. They also had given me my new number. I was now 98.

When I got back to the hotel that afternoon, I called Kabeer.

"You got cut," was the first thing he said.

"No," I said, hardly believing the words coming out of my mouth, "I made the team."

I spent the rest of the day sitting on my hotel bed, just looking out the window and thinking. I thought a lot about my mother and what she would say if she were there, and how sad I was that I couldn't call her. I thought about my high school coach, Robert Garrett, who saw something in me when all I could see was basketball. "But I'm a basketball player!" I had said defiantly. I thought about how my Achilles tendon injury nearly ended my career three years earlier. And how, four months earlier, I had been gripped with fear, followed swiftly by despair, on Draft Day. I thought, and I thought. About everything, every moment and person that had led me to that point in my life.

I was in the NFL. I had made it.

Then panic gripped me, and my next thought was: *Oh, shoot, where am I going to live?*

THE FEAR THAT STOPS US

When many of us start out on our journey toward our dreams, we don't think much about fear. At least, we don't think that fear itself is anything to worry about. What some of us are afraid of is whether we have what it takes to do what we want to do. Either we think that we simply won't be good enough or we don't have those intangibles—we lack discipline, determination, or heart. We think that our initial jolt of motivation and energy is going to gradually give way to laziness and apathy. We think that maybe we'll lose our passion and get distracted by other interests and pursuits. We think that maybe we don't have "it"—that formless quality that allows others to be great, but not us.

I had plenty of self-doubt growing up. But rather than let that doubt consume me, it fueled my determination, which was never in short supply. I have always been very good at using setbacks as motivation. When I was younger, I used the criticism of others to push me ahead. No one likes being seen as not good enough, but I learned to turn their doubt into a burning fire inside me. "You don't think I'll do it? Just watch!"

I realize that I was also helped by my career choice. Being an athlete for as long as I can remember, trying to "make the team" was like second nature to me. When you're an athlete, you're always trying out in some form or another. Starters can lose their spot; rookies can outshine veterans; and injuries are just one play away from ending a game, a season, or a career. Sometimes you're the one who must step aside for another, and sometimes you're the one taking their place. In sports, those who don't overcome their fears and rise to the occasion don't last. You're always under the microscope; you're always being tested.

But not everyone has had my experience. A lot of people don't live a life where they're always "trying out." Some of the ninjas you meet in this book had never been athletes before. So when they embark on the path of an athlete, they don't bring the same frame of mind that a professional athlete might bring. A professional is used to not making the team or not being good enough. That doesn't mean it's easy to accept, but that's part of our world. Nonathletes might find the need to rise to the occasion a terrifying experience. The job promotion that seems too big a leap—the opportunity that would require hours away from the famiy, the business start-up that would force you to dip into your savings—these are occasions that might excite us, because they hold the promise of fulfilling our dreams, yet they also scare us, because they put us out there, exposed and vulnerable.

And that's what I mean about fear. It's not the fear of lacking something. It's the fear of success. That probably sounds strange. Isn't that what we want to do: succeed? Yes, but ask yourself why so many people don't succeed. Most people have dreams and goals. A lot of people want to achieve something great. Few do. It's not because they failed at it. Instead, when the moment came . . . they backed down. They weren't afraid of failure; they were afraid of success.

Why would anyone be afraid of success? Because success comes with exposure; you're out there, and now you must sustain this level of excellence. You feel like you must keep achieving at a high level—and that's an exhausting thought. It's so much safer being mediocre. No one expects anything. You don't have to put yourself on the line. What's so great about greatness, anyway? Why would you leave this zone of comfort that you've lived in to dangle in the wind, where you could fail or disappoint?

A lot of people prefer to stay in the comfortable middle, right where no one expects anything of them. If you can minimize the expectation of you, then you don't need to look over your shoulder. There's no one trying to take your spot on the roster. There's no one pushing you to elevate your game. If you've been pursuing your dream, and suddenly find yourself face-to-face with its realization, this is when you start to backpedal. This is when you start to procrastinate and blame your lack of discipline or motivation. Consciously or not, you start to see the way you were before you tried to pursue your dream as acceptable. At least there was no pressure, no one to live up to.

And that's how we sabotage ourselves. It doesn't matter when it happens—either during training or right before the big game—we make the decision that it's better to stay where we are. It's better to stay with who we are. Greatness is hard; mediocrity is so easy. Why go through all that physical and mental anguish and self-doubt when you can just be what you've always been?

I think a lot of us know someone who backed down from an opportunity. I certainly do. They were given a chance of a lifetime, and they walked away. We scream at them, "Why? This is what you wanted, right?" They mumble something like, "It's not the right fit for me," or "I don't want all that pressure." They want you to forget all the dreams and aspirations they talked about before the opportunity presented itself. They want you to forget because they need to forget it too.

To pursue your dreams, to chase greatness, is a trial. It's a test of character, strength, and will. It's not meant to be easy. When some of us discover that, we give up on that dream we had cherished. Fear can be your greatest enemy. Discipline, determination, will—they all flow from an acceptance that you will succeed in your journey or die trying. That must be the attitude one takes into this fight for greatness.

A NEW CAREER, A NEW FEAR

I mentioned that I was never really afraid of success as an athlete. Some of it had to do with the idea that I was always chasing someone better in my long journey in sports. I was never the greatest, and I found my motivation in proving that I belonged. You don't make the NFL if you have a fear of performing at the top of your game. No one in the NFL—no one who starts in college—would be there if they had.

But I've known fear elsewhere in my career. When I left sports, I left the only thing I really knew well. I knew what it meant to be part of a team. You commit yourself to a team and you commit yourself to your teammates. That's a very tough bond to break. It propels you to do things you probably couldn't do on your own. Iron sharpens iron, as they say. But when I left the NFL, I left team sports behind. I was on my own, and it was scary. There was no one to chase anymore.

Broadcasting wasn't a new venture for me. I know that it might seem like a predictable career path for a former athlete, but I had been interested in broadcasting and entertainment since I was a boy. Don't tell anyone, but when I was younger I would tape every episode of *The Oprah Winfrey Show*. Go ahead, laugh. But I loved what Oprah could do on that stage, in that chair, channeling her emotional intelligence, grace, and good humor to get her guests to talk and discuss what matters in life. (I also watched *General Hospital*, but the less about that the better.)

I was drawn to the fact that Oprah was a successful black woman who was able to elicit such emotion and happiness in her audience. She drew me in, just with the way she spoke. I felt the same when I saw Denzel Washington in *Malcolm X*—another black person whose power with language was power itself. These were great icons for a black kid in South Central Los Angeles to look up to. Yes, I had my athletic idols too, like Muhammad Ali, but again, Ali fascinated me because he could command an audience. When Ali spoke, people listened. When Malcolm X spoke, people heard. When Oprah spoke, people felt. As a child, my mother saw my interest in language and told me I would be a good pastor.

Despite my focus on athletics, I always knew I needed another game plan, something that I could do if professional sports didn't work out for me. Even though I focused on sports, I didn't let this other passion sit unattended. I might not have followed my father's advice to "learn a trade," at least not right away, but I never forgot it. When I went to college, I considered my major in a deeper way than most athletes. The NFL wasn't even a dream yet when I was a freshman, and I knew that I needed to focus on my education. I had been given the gift of a scholarship and I wasn't going to waste it.

I looked at a business management major—nope, too much math—then I considered criminal justice, a major that most athletes pursued (mostly because it isn't terribly difficult to graduate with that degree in four years). But my mind went straight to my other childhood passion—communications. My counselors tried to talk me out of it. SDSU has a popular and demanding communications department. To get a degree in that field, I would need to work hard, regardless of my athletic pursuits.

I didn't mind. I had an image in my head of what I wanted to do after sports, and that path went through communications. I wanted to be in front of an audience, on-screen, using my words like my idols used them, to heighten the viewing experience with what I said and how I said it. Once again, my Achilles tendon injury turned into a blessing in disguise because I was able to focus on my studies during my period away from football. I got the best grades of my life while I had a cast on my leg. And I succeeded in graduating in four years, got my degree in communications, and felt prepared if my NFL dreams went up in smoke.

They didn't, and I spent six years as a professional football player. But I never entirely ignored my other passion. In 2007, during my fourth year in the league, the NFL started a "Broadcast Bootcamp," which was an intensive two-week course that helped current players learn a bit about the broadcasting industry. Applicants had to submit an essay explaining their reasons for wanting to participate. I had just been cut by the Dolphins (on September 10) and was a free agent, meaning technically I was still in the league and eligible for the boot camp. So I applied. Here's a portion of what I wrote, which gives an idea of how I never, even in the middle of my playing years, let my broadcasting dreams slip too far from my mind:

> *Throughout my collegiate and professional football career, I have participated in various aspects of sports broadcasting. I served as an NFL analyst for the 2006 season on Sirius Satellite Radio (NFL Radio) and provided analysis for a variety of games and player matchups. In addition, I worked as a color analyst for Channel 4 San Diego during a game between the University of San Diego and Morehead State University. As a color analyst, I was able to combine my experience as a football player along with educational tools to provide analysis of the game. Lastly, I have worked as a guest cohost for Fox 6 San Diego's* That Sunday Night Sport Show. *The majority of my off-season time has been spent educating myself with the skills necessary to succeed in sports broadcasting.*

Hundreds applied for the boot camp, but only twenty were accepted. I was one of them. The boot camp was only a week, and participants divided their time between in-studio work and field reporting. So, for instance, one day I might find myself sitting across from James Brown, the famed football host who now anchors CBS's Sunday NFL coverage, and the next day reporting from Dick's Sporting Goods. We got practice calling games as well, which would prove invaluable to the jobs I would take later. They'd gather us around a television and replay old broadcasts, like an old Super Bowl game, but without the commentary. We were supposed to provide the commentary. At the end of the week, they'd hand you your "tape," which was a compilation of all the footage you had acquired, and you'd meet with a panel of judges who'd critique your performance. It was tough, but great fun and extremely helpful.

I needed that confidence, because when I left the NFL a year later, I discovered a painful reality about life after football. A lot of the guys you call teammates suddenly stop being your friends. These were guys you bled with, fought with, lost with, and won with. During your days together on the team—or even if you're on different teams—you would do anything for them, and they for you.

And then you're cut. Then things change. The same guys who would do anything for a teammate or former teammates suddenly don't answer your calls anymore. The only thing worse than the pain of getting cut is the sting that comes with knowing you've been cast out of the club. Some of the other players just don't want to associate with a guy who left the league because he was cut. I can remember few lonelier moments in my life than those months after I was cut.

I also was going through the pain of realizing that I had not had the football career I had wanted. I just felt like I should have done more. But when you're an out-of-work athlete, you don't have the luxury of wallowing in your own regret and self-pity. I knew what I wanted to do, I just had no clue about how to do it.

That might sound strange. I was a former NFL athlete; how hard could it be to get a job in broadcasting? That seems to be a traditional, and well-trod, path for guys like me. Surely I could get a start calling college football games. That is true, for the former players who were great. Look at the guys who are calling games on Sunday, or even doing commentary on the cable networks. If you're an NFL fan, you knew these guys when they were players. Almost all of them were great. These players are hired because their greatness legitimizes their commentary and analysis. They're Hall-of-Famers, Super Bowl champions, Pro-Bowlers.

Then there's me. I was none of those things. I had to start at the bottom, and it was a very deep bottom. I had no platform to lean on or really any connections to get me a start. The entertainment world, I swiftly discovered, is even harsher than the sports world when it comes to relationships. I had none and I was acutely aware of it through lack of interest from possible employers.

And that's when I met C. S. Keys. I knew Keys because he was one of the top sports anchors in San Diego, and his career reflects the discipline and determination he put into his craft. Keys started as a weatherman for a local news station before working his way up to sports anchor at San Diego's Fox affiliate. Keys also hosted a weekly Sunday show in town, aptly named *The Sunday Sports Show*, and had his own radio programs.

In the world of San Diego sports, C. S. Keys was the man. I made a point of scheduling a meeting with C.S. I wanted to pick his brain about this brave new world I had the courage (or stupidity) to break into. Sometimes, all you need to do is make the ask. I did. Keys happily accepted my offer to get together. And then he did something I didn't expect: he told me he would have me on his show anytime I wanted.

I would end up cutting my broadcasting teeth sitting next to C. S. Keys, giving analysis and insights on the latest Chargers game or bit of news. Of course, I was terrible at first. I fumbled over my words, I didn't have the right head bobs and gesticulations. You don't think of these things when you're talking sports with your friends. But doing it in front of the camera, it's a whole different experience. For a beginner like me, it's unnatural.

And still I couldn't quite get it.

"You know what you need to do?" C.S. told me one day. "You need to take acting lessons."

And so I did. I learned how to get comfortable in front of an audience. I learned how to talk and move in a way that wasn't distracting for the viewer. I still wasn't great at it, but I was learning. And I owed it all to C. S. Keys, my first mentor in the broadcasting world.

This was a terrifying moment in my life, but I had the wisdom—the courage—to reach out and ask for help. Keys accepted, and helped me break into an industry I otherwise might have been shut out of. That's the thing about asking for help—it can open doors. We can find an opportunity that we would otherwise never get. The terrible truth about broadcasting is that you need a tape—basically a highlight reel of you talking to the camera—to get a job. But you need a job to get a tape. The open invitation C.S. gave me allowed me to put together that desperately needed highlight reel. I still had a long road ahead, but at least I had started the journey. I don't know where I'd be without C. S. Keys, but I certainly wouldn't be where I am now.

As an athlete, I learned to get by on my skill. It wasn't a question of knowing the right person; I was either good enough or I wasn't. But when I left athletics, I entered a different world. It's one you probably know well; the one where connections matter, where a network matters. If you don't have connections or much of a network, then your chances of walking in the front door are slim.

So overcome your fear and go through the back door. That was the lesson I learned from C. S. Keys. When I found the front doors of broadcasting shut to me—even as someone who had spent six years in the NFL—C. S. Keys let me in the back way. He was a mentor to me in the traditional sense; he taught me a lot about how to be a better broadcaster *and* entertainer. But he also gave me a lucky break.

Except it wasn't lucky. Or, rather, I define luck as "preparation meeting opportunity." I had been preparing myself to ask for help. So when the opportunity presented itself I was prepared to pursue someone who could teach me. Stop being afraid, and start preparing yourself for when an opportunity might let you in the back door.

There's a catch, though. We all know those people in our life who are the "climbers"; they're great at meeting the right people and using them for their connections. I'm not telling you to use anyone. I didn't know C.S. would give me so many opportunities to practice and improve my broadcasting skills on his show. I asked him for advice: *What should I do?* Not: *What can you do for me?*

I know the world runs on favors, and to dismiss this fact of life is naïve. But I also know that it's easy to spot those people who are only out for themselves, who use others to get a leg up. They're transparent and they stink of opportunism. We find a way to achieve our dreams, but we don't give up our basic decency. I've been on the other end of it.

Match your courage with decency and you'll find those locked doors open up. Or you will be shown the back door.

THE COURAGE TO SUCCEED

Early in my broadcasting career, I managed to schedule an interview with ESPN up in Bristol, Connecticut. The big leagues!

During the interview, I sat down with two company executives. I was new to the whole "job interview" game, but I had on my best suit and I felt ready. I was brimming with confidence. Then one of the executives asks me: "What makes you different?"

That's when I said it: "I'm just like Stuart Scott."

For those who don't know, Stuart Scott, who passed away tragically in 2015, was a sportscasting legend. Along with other early ESPN broadcasters like Dan Patrick and Chris Berman, Scott was one of the original modern sports anchors: irreverent, humorous, and funny as hell. Scott wasn't just an anchor reading the news; he was his own character. Viewers tuned in to watch Scott probably more than they cared about the news Scott reported.

In other words, it's as if I had answered the question of "How smart are you?" with "I'm just like Albert Einstein." It was a bad move.

One of the executives leaned in and said, "Let me tell you something: We have a Stuart Scott. We don't need a Stuart Scott."

They let me off easy. There was no reason to beat around the bush; I wasn't going to be on ESPN. But they gave me some advice to send me on my way back to San Diego: They told me I needed more "tape," the industry term for relevant experience. They also told me something very humbling, but also critically important. They said that there were hundreds of guys just like me—former athletes trying to get into broadcasting—who were better than me and *they* would never be hired by ESPN. Talk about keeping it real. They didn't say I should find another line of work; they just said I wasn't ready and that it was going to be a hard road ahead.

It was tough to hear, but they were right. Like with so many setbacks, I now see that ESPN interview in a different light. At the time, I was embarrassed and scared out of my mind. Was I doing the right thing? Did I have a shot at *this* dream? But now, after learning a lot more about this business, I know they did me a huge favor. If, by some miracle, they would have put me in front of a camera, I would've stunk. Not just that, but I would've stunk on one of the biggest broadcasting stages in the industry.

It's hard to recover from that sort of failure. There's the professional stigma that would have been attached to me wherever I went: "Oh, you're the guy who lasted three seconds on ESPN? Don't call us; we'll call you." There's also the personal devastation, the shattering of confidence—the very confidence that one so desperately needs to be good in front of the camera. I had the confidence I had gathered from my brief broadcasting experience while still a player. I thought it was enough. Only when I had more experience did I learn that it wasn't.

In any case, I got the message. I spent the next several years calling college football games on the Mtn. Network and then for CBS College Sports Network. In 2012, I got an audition with NFL Network for its *Fantasy Live* show. Less than a year later, in early 2013, my agent called me to ask if I wanted to audition to be the host of *American Ninja Warrior*.

My response? "American Ninja what?" Of course, I didn't say that, but the truth is that I didn't know the show. Instead, I told him I loved the show and that I would be honored to audition. Then I went to watch a few episodes. What I saw blew me away and I was instantly hooked. Everything about the struggle of the athletes and their backstories inspired me. I'm still inspired by it all to this day. I would learn to draw on that inspiration later and fine-tune how I call the show.

At first, I really didn't know what the producers expected of me. My thoughts immediately turned to a childhood passion of mine, WWE. The spectacle of *Ninja Warrior*, the larger-than-life characters and the crazy things they had to do, reminded me of professional wrestling. I remember how I loved the commentary, the over-the-top, this-guy-can't-be-that-excited exuberance of it all. I felt like I could do that. After all, I was the child of two Nigerians, who came from a culture where exaggeration is just part of talking. Nigerians get animated about everything. My mother, who would watch WWE with me, would joke that Hulk Hogan was her husband. The Hulkster would get in the ring, tear away his shirt, and my mother would scream: "That's my husband! That's my husband!"

In any case, that's what I decided to bring to my audition— WWE, with some Nigerian flair. The producers had me call a few runs with Matt Iseman and I did my best. That was it, and I left not expecting anything. You only need to be in the entertainment world a short time before you learn to keep your expectations low. It takes only a few total heartbreaks to know that you need to develop a thick skin in this business. I had auditioned for other high-profile shows before, so it wasn't as if I was naïve about my chances.

I auditioned for the show in late February, and you can imagine my surprise when my agent called me back on March 25, 2013, and told me I was going to be the new cohost of *American Ninja Warrior*. I was in shock. You go to auditions, do your best, then forget them. I didn't think I had the experience or the talent to cohost such a hugely popular show, and I certainly didn't pin my self-esteem on it. You almost become numb to the entire process. Another audition, and another, and another. You don't worry about getting called back because you're already at the next audition. So when that call came, I panicked. My first thought was: *I'm not ready for this.*

Yet here it was, and the big leagues of TV wanted me. I was being called up. The dream was being realized, the one that I had dared to imagine when I left my NFL career, full of regret and resentment. I had told myself I would reach new heights, that I would conquer a new profession. I just didn't think I was so close to the summit.

And that's why I know about fear. I had the opportunity handed to me, and I almost backed down. I was afraid. I had pursued my broadcasting and entertainment dreams so methodically that I was used to performing in a very specific way: calling games and giving some color commentary. *Fantasy Live* had allowed me to experiment and hone a bigger stage presence, a more unique on-camera personality. But I didn't feel like any of my previous experience had prepared me for the enormity of *Ninja Warrior*.

I had just started to become comfortable in the world I was in. I was enjoying my time at the NFL Network, happy to have a regular gig that didn't take me all over the country calling college football games. And I had developed a strong sense that "my time would come, but not yet." That's an easy place to hang out—doing what you love but *not quite* at the level you want to be.

Getting ready for greatness is a safe state of mind. You don't need to fear too much about failure or not living up to expectations. You can just sort of coast along.

Why give that up? Why diverge from the comfortable "getting ready for greatness" path onto a road full of dangers and uncertainty, the greatest of all being: What if I stink? What if I was right, that I wasn't ready for *Ninja Warrior*? What if I fell flat on my face? Could my career survive such a failure? Could I survive such a devastating humiliation? The lesson I learned from my ESPN interview came back to haunt me big-time.

What I said earlier about others I can now say for myself. I was afraid of success. I was terrified of greatness. And I know why others balk when the opportunity for greatness comes calling. I, who had never missed a chance to prove myself, found myself on the edge of self-sabotage.

PURPOSE DEFEATS FEAR

So how did I overcome it? Why do you see me doing my thing on *American Ninja Warrior* if I was so deathly afraid of success?

I said yes to *American Ninja Warrior* because, despite my fear, I remembered what I wanted out of life. I have always kept my goals very clear in my mind, and my broadcasting/entertainment goal was no different. I reminded myself that my path toward success had never been easy. My journey to the NFL didn't go through the draft; I had to find another way in. My path to a steady broadcasting career didn't start how I imagined: I wasn't handed a job out of the NFL, based on the little experience I had and my status as a former player. I had to start from the bottom. I had to remind myself that our journeys toward success—mine, at least—had never followed the path I had originally intended to pursue.

To refuse a different path than the one I had in mind went against everything I had learned in my life. It was when I had to go down those dark roads, grapple with my fears, that I found success. Maybe this opportunity was no different. We often can't choose our paths, but we always have a say in where they end. My ambition, my dream, was clear in my mind. When faced with my fear of hosting *American Ninja Warrior*, I had that memory— that this is something I had wanted since childhood—to fall back on. I was able to arrest my fall into self-sabotage by remembering what I had been working toward for five years, since leaving the NFL. Maybe I wasn't ready and maybe I wasn't good enough, but I couldn't say no. Saying no, giving in to my fear, would have been a betrayal, and not just of my own ambition. It would have been a betrayal to everyone who had helped me get to that moment—from C. S. Keys to my own wife.

Dreams are more than wishes, although we sometimes confuse the two. We have dreams because we want to find our purpose in life. Now, we can have more than one purpose—I am first and foremost a father and husband. That is and always will be my greatest purpose. But when we talk about our professional and personal dreams, what we should be saying is: This is what God wants me to do, who God wants me to be. Therefore, our dreams are our calling; they are what we are here to do. Even if I wasn't the greatest NFL player, my career in the NFL was a meaningful pursuit. There was a purpose for me to play in the NFL. There is a purpose for me to be the cohost of *American Ninja Warrior*.

Fear stands no chance when up against purpose. That is what I've learned. Where I am in my professional career is exactly where I am supposed to be. I've always been able to see the end. I got here by walking through that dark scary door with the sign overhead that read "You're Not Ready." I closed my eyes and walked through, because that's what I was supposed to do. My decade-long pursuit of broadcasting, which had begun in college and continued throughout my NFL days, wasn't an accident. Where you are in your journey isn't an accident either. But there comes a moment when we must walk through that dark door, past the fear of the unfamiliar, and keep moving forward, confident that we are headed in the right direction.

THE FEAR OF EXPECTATIONS

To the outsider, Allyson Felix's story is one of perpetual triumphs. She has won nine Olympic medals (six golds), which is tied for the record for the most medals won by a female Olympian in track and field. By any measurement, Allyson Felix has achieved greatness.

I first met Allyson Felix through our work together on my friend and former teammate Nnamdi Asomugha's foundation. The Asomugha Foundation seeks to provide educational opportunities for disadvantaged youth and women, a cause that both Allyson and I share. In the years that I've gotten to know Allyson, I've discovered more than just an astounding athlete. She's a woman who has overcome tremendous failures and fears in her life. Her road might be paved with Olympic medals, but it was a long, hard road for Allyson.

Like me, Allyson started down her athletic career with a passion for basketball. It was only during her sophomore year in high school, when she was trying to fit in at a new school, that her father and brother, runners themselves, encouraged her to try out for the track team to make friends.

"My career started much later than most Olympic athletes," she told me. "By the time a runner is in high school, they've usually been doing the sport for several years, since grade school."

Her new teammates, although realizing Allyson's potential, gave her the nickname "Chicken Legs." Allyson didn't love it. At five feet six, 125 pounds, Allyson's skinny appearance masked her tremendous strength. The name stuck, however, and in time Allyson proved to her teammates that appearances don't matter. By her senior year, Allyson had been named High School Athlete of the Year by *Track & Field News*. Graduating in 2003, Allyson caused a bit of controversy when she signed a contract with Adidas, which would make her ineligible to compete at the college level. But Allyson had her sights set beyond college. Besides, part of the deal with Adidas was that the company would pay for her tuition. College was an educational venture for Allyson. She would pursue her athletic dreams outside college.

Allyson competed in her first Olympics at the 2004 Summer Games in Athens. She won the silver in the 200 meters. She was just eighteen. How does an eighteen-year-old handle that kind of pressure?

"At the beginning I didn't realize there was pressure," she told me. She was a kid, a bit overwhelmed at the moment and the stage, but also just happy to be there.

Between Olympics, she won golds at the World Championships and the IAFF World Championships in Athletics. Everything was all set to capture the gold in the 200 meters in Beijing in 2008.

Except she didn't. The expectations for Allyson before Beijing couldn't have been higher. She had fans, sponsors, her teammates, an entire nation rooting for her—and assuming she'd come home with the gold. Her youth and inexperience had put Allyson on the media's radar after Athens; now she was the seasoned veteran, a favorite, anything but an underdog. Someone who was supposed to win. That's a scary place to be. "My second Olympics, pressure became real to me," she said.

Allyson placed second, again losing to the 2004 gold medalist, Veronica Campbell of Jamaica. "It was a failure, but it was also the biggest lesson I ever learned."

What did she learn?

"I was at my lowest point," she says, looking back. "I still wanted to run, but I had so little motivation left. Could I do this? I was just frustrated with the sport in general."

After the Games, she felt like her career was over. Or at least that it should be over. She had failed on the world's biggest track stage and the thought of climbing up that mountain again seemed too much. It wasn't so much a question of whether she would get back to the Olympics, but if she wanted to get back. It was during this period that Allyson said she relied on her support system—her coach, her friends, and her teammates—to help her see what she couldn't: that she was meant to be great. She listened to them, not the fears in her own heart. And she threw herself back into training. With her coach by her side, she examined everything—her training regimen, her eating habits, the people she was training with. It all had to be rejiggered to help Allyson get to where she wanted to be—as well as erase those fears that almost drove her from the sport.

When the 2012 Summer Games in London approached, Allyson could say: "I was confident there was nothing left to be done. I felt so at peace." She said she had "done everything" she could to prepare for the Games. The rest was in God's hands.

In London, Allyson ran four events: the 100 meters, the 200 meters, the 4x100 meters, and the 4x400 meters. She got fifth in the 100 meters. She won gold in the other three, matching Florence Griffith-Joyner's three golds from the 1988 Games in Seoul.

Four years later, another setback, this time an ankle injury right before the 2016 Games in Rio de Janeiro. Her goal was to win four golds, although she had switched from the 100 meters to the 400 meters. Now? "Everything I had worked so hard for was just gone," she says, looking back. "I couldn't train. I couldn't even walk for a while. At the same time, I'm still doing advertisements and promotions for the Games, which were three months away."

The old fears came roaring back. She was going to fail on the big stage. She wasn't going to live up to the expectations of others and herself. If the expectations had been high for Beijing, they were astronomical for Rio. There was a precedent for the fears Allyson had felt. Before the 1992 Games in Barcelona, Reebok had invested heavily in a marketing campaign centered on American decathletes Dan O'Brien and Dave Johnson. The campaign kicked off months before, so early in fact that neither O'Brien nor Johnson had even qualified for the Games yet. Each commercial would show the two competitors training and competing against each other and end with this line: "Who will be the world's greatest athlete—Dan or Dave? To be settled this summer in Barcelona." But O'Brien failed to qualify for the Olympics, and Johnson finished third in the decathlon at the Games.

While Allyson's pre-Games endorsements didn't match the tone of the "Dan and Dave" campaign—sponsors had learned their lesson—they still put a tremendous amount of pressure on Allyson. And now she was injured. Could she come back?

"I had the same feeling of despair after my second Olympics," she remembers. "But, just like then, my support group stepped up."

Allyson also fell back on another factor that had been with her for her whole life: her faith. Her father was a pastor and had instilled in Allyson a passion for Christ.

"It's only natural that my faith would spill into my athletic career. My talent is a gift from God. Knowing that helps me put things into perspective a lot of the time. It's so easy to get consumed with winning. But that's not what this is all about; this is bigger than medals. I use my gift for God's glory."

And that's how she found the courage to overcome her fears. It wasn't about winning; it was about using God's gift. The expectations; the gold medals; the endorsements—they were secondary to what really mattered. She would use her gift and compete. That's what she was meant to do.

However, the injury kept Allyson from competing in any professional meets before the Olympic Trials in Eugene, Oregon. She missed qualifying for the 200 meters but won the 400 meters and earned a spot on both the 4x100 meter and 4x400 meter relay teams. At Rio, Allyson won golds in both relay events but missed first place in the 400 meters by 0.07 seconds. Her opponent, Shaunae Miller of the Bahamas, dove across the finish line at the last possible second.

It was a disappointment, but Allyson no longer sees disappointments as failures. She doesn't run for medals. She runs for friends, for family, for God, and for herself. That's how you overcome your fear: you ignore what others expect and do it because it's what you were meant to do.

Allyson knows that her ability is a gift from God, Who wants her to compete. And it was because of her purpose to serve God that she overcame her fear of not competing well enough. While I competed at the highest levels of football, I didn't achieve the success that Allyson has achieved on the track. Since first meeting her, I have been awed by her tenacity and optimism. Allyson taught me that fear is just another obstacle to overcome. But also, that the way to overcome it is not to give in to it.

6

SIT IN YOUR FAILURE

E ven NFL players get the Monday blues. On Monday morning, the entire team sits in one room and the coaches go play-by-play from the previous game, picking apart everyone's mistakes. Imagine that every week your boss brings together the whole office and says, "We're going to talk about every one of your screwups last week." It's humiliating. And you will never feel smaller than when fifty-two of your teammates are all looking at you because of your boneheaded play.

In my second year in the league, we played the Colts, who were then under the leadership of the great Peyton Manning. We got whupped, losing 35–14. The next day, during Monday-morning film, I knew what was coming, and, boy, it came. At a critical fourth and short, I had jumped offside, giving the Colts a first down. Now, guys jump offside. It happens. But everything about my penalty was embarrassing. Manning had "hard counted" us, meaning he had emphasized parts of his snap count by raising his voice to make it seem like the ball was about to be snapped. Even if Manning was one of the best hard counters in the game, it's an old trick, and one I should've anticipated. But I was fired up and lost my focus. Manning hard counts, I jump, Colts get the first, and everyone is looking at me. It's hard enough to deal with that shame during the game; it's miserable to relive it the next day.

"We must be the dumbest team in the league," I remember our head coach saying. Using my penalty as an example, he continued to shout. "This is undisciplined football!"

I wanted to crawl into a corner. For a player like me, whose position was never secure, mistakes like that are the ones that get you cut. I had the feeling that my career was over. Like I said, Monday-morning film—the worst day of the week.

But you know something? I don't think I ever jumped offside again in my career. At least I don't remember doing so. I would have been ashamed of my penalty even if Coach hadn't called it out the next day. But by calling it out, in front of everyone, I had to live it again. I had to sit in my failure. I wasn't allowed to forget it, like I wanted to do. I had to own it.

In the NFL, and in most of sports, owning failure is part of the game. Everyone messes up. Even guys like Manning, whose own fumbles, interceptions, and misthrows were shown on Monday morning just like everybody else's.

There's a reason for this. Coaches don't call out a player's failures because they like humiliating them, but humiliation is the goal. They do it because it leads to results. It works. It works because a guy will do almost anything to avoid repeating that humiliating experience again. It's not the penalty itself that leads to the humiliation; it's sitting in a room with your teammates, being told you let them down. That's some tough medicine.

Fans might think that players are tough enough to handle criticism. We are, but that's only because we learn how to handle it. We have had to sit in our failures since we were playing ball in high school, where the mentality is no different than in the NFL. You're humiliated, you sit in it, then you get better.

DON'T WATER DOWN FAILURE

Failure hurts so much that we, as a society, have tried to minimize its impact. Kids are told that it's okay to fail. We read how great men and women failed time and again. We're told that failure is a part of life and it's nothing to get upset about. At the same time, we're told to learn from our mistakes. How can we learn from our failures and mistakes if we're told that they're no big deal?

You can't really have it both ways. It is the pain that makes failure a step toward success. By trying to hide your failure or minimize it, what you're really doing is protecting your own ego at the expense of improvement. We don't get stronger by giving our muscles a little bit of a workout—nothing too painful, nice and steady. We get stronger when we literally shred our muscle fibers, so that when they grow back, they grow back larger. It's the trauma, the pain, that builds our bodies. It's no different when we're going after our dreams. Experiencing the pain of failure helps us grow.

When I wasn't drafted, I felt the sting of failure unlike anything I had known before. What helped pull me back and refocus my mind was something my father would say. Growing up, I always felt like I couldn't impress him. "Hey, Dad, I graduated high school! Aren't you proud?" His response: "You must graduate college." That's my father. He didn't hand out accolades for accomplishments that only took you halfway. Nothing about my achievements in college guaranteed I would make the NFL. But I had started to believe that I would always get by, because I had worked hard.

Despite my euphoria at making the Raiders, I was always "on the bubble," as they say, meaning I was always in danger of getting cut. Things got worse for me when, in my second season, the team hired Rob Ryan from New England, fresh off its Super Bowl victory. A linebacker coach at New England, Ryan shifted the structure of the Oakland defense from a 4–3 to a 3–4. Not to get too technical, but the numbers refer to (1) how many down linemen there are, and (2) how many linebackers there are. So in a 4–3, the scheme I had played most of my career, there are four down linemen and three linebackers. The scheme emphasizes the role of the defensive end. But in a 3–4, the defensive end is replaced with an outside linebacker, who might rush the passer or fall into pass coverage. I had spent my rookie year learning the 4–3, a scheme I had known from college, but the game is so much faster in the NFL. Plays develop almost instantly, leaving a defender with little time to react. In the NFL, a player must react on instinct. He must be able to see how the play will develop before it develops. Sometimes he guesses wrong, but if you don't develop those instincts—if you don't make the game slow down for you—then you won't last in the NFL. With my position never secure, I poured myself into studying the defense, learning my assignments, knowing exactly where I was supposed to be when I was supposed to be there. I had worked all off-season on getting better—in a 4–3 defense.

Then, whoop! It all went out the window. It was as if I were a rookie again.

Ryan moved me from defensive end to outside linebacker. To even think about succeeding at that position, I had to drop from my rookie weight of 270 to 250. That was hard enough; but learning the game all over again was a whole other thing. The truth of the matter is that I didn't excel at my new position. I had to learn coverage schemes and route combinations. Ryan was a good coach—one of the best in the game—but he expected his players to pick it up quickly. I struggled mightily.

I got through my second year under the new Ryan scheme, despite my blunder during the game against Manning, but my self-doubt had come roaring back. By the time my third season rolled around, I had to admit that I still didn't quite grasp the linebacker position. I went into the final preseason game of the year, against the New Orleans Saints, with little doubt about what was going to happen. How? The coaches stopped screaming at me. It sounds counterintuitive, but I never forgot what my father would tell me when I got upset after my high school coach chewed me out.

"He screams because he cares."

Coaches won't blow their vocal cords at a guy on his way out. They let him play it out. That's how I knew. I was a "dead man walking," the term we adopted from death row. I fought against the "woe is me" attitude and continued to play. That's one of the toughest battles one can face. We sometimes think that failure will be a one-time thing that happens *after* we've put in all the work and energy. But failure can also be happening *while* you're still working. You know you're failing but you can't quit.

I still gave my all that game and dropped to the ground in exhaustion afterward.

Two days later, I was having breakfast at my favorite spot in Alameda, California, when I got the call. No hiding behind locker room doors this time. "Hey, Akbar, Coach needs to see you." You can expect something and still be shocked when it happens. That was me at that moment. I knew my failure to embrace the linebacker position had jeopardized my spot on the team. I had tried to mask my inadequacies with hustle, by leaving it all out there. But the NFL isn't like the movie *Rudy*; you don't get a gold star for hustle.

Getting cut hurt, but the pain was different from when I wasn't drafted. I was more mature. I had just bought a house and a new BMW—things that I could only dream about when in college. But even though I had "made the NFL," a two-year career was not what I had had in mind. The sting of failure got worse when I couldn't catch on with any team during that 2005 season. I had team workouts with Green Bay (where my brother was kill-ing it), Houston, and Dallas, where Coach Bill Parcells was none too subtle in telling me I couldn't play for him.

Wow, I thought. *Is this it? Two years and done?*

I had the rest of the season to ponder that question. Or so I thought. I went home to San Diego and spent week after week frustrated that I wasn't playing. I would work out, spend time with my family and friends, and try to get through my days without feeling like a total failure. And occasionally go to a team tryout—only to be miserable afterward when they wouldn't sign me. My tryout with Green Bay was particularly demoralizing. They had invited a bunch of free agents to come try out with the team, each one being told through the course of the day that they weren't needed. By the end of the day, I was the last one standing. I dared to hope, even calling up Kabeer to let him know that we might be teammates again. But then the ax fell, and I was back home in San Diego. My phone wasn't ringing, and I started to seriously accept that my NFL career was over. Then one day toward the end of the season I woke up, as usual, although something had changed. I wasn't going to take this lying down. I was going to act. If I go down fighting, then at least I knew I fought. I hopped out of bed and threw on my Jordan sweater and blue Nike sweatpants. It was early, but I wanted to get to the San Diego Chargers' clubhouse before the coaches did. When I arrived, I walked straight up to the receptionist, Georgette.

"I'm here to meet with Marty Schottenheimer [then the Chargers' head coach]," I declared.

The smile she gave me said, "I'm sure you are," but the words she spoke were: "Is he expecting you?"

"No," I said, honestly. "I was cut from the Raiders and I want to play for the Chargers."

Another smile. "Okay, I'll pass this along."

I was dismissed. I'm forward, but I know when to leave a party. So I thanked her and turned to leave, when who do I see walking into the building? Coach Schottenheimer.

God is good.

"Hey, Coach, my name is Akbar Gbaja—"

"I know who you are," said Marty.

"Well, Coach, I'd love to be a part of the Chargers," I began.

"Okay, let me speak to my staff and we'll get back to you," he said, before walking by.

I didn't know what to make of it. Was it a polite brush-off? Would he talk to his staff?

All I knew is that I had done what I could. I even managed to speak to the coach himself. It was now in God's—and the Chargers'—hands. The season ended a month or so later. Then I got the callback early in 2006. The Chargers wanted me to come to OTAs (which is short for organized team activities) in March—without a tryout. I ended up not making the team, but I got a callback from the team midseason. One of their top linebackers had been suspended, and they needed me to fill his slot. I jumped at the chance. I played for six weeks. Then, a day before a game in Buffalo, I was walking back to the locker room when I ran into Coach Schottenheimer. He wanted to tell me himself that they were going to let me go. The suspended player was returning, and it was a simple numbers thing. I was devastated, I even cried, but I respected Marty for what he did—from

the moment I ambushed him in his office to the moment he told me personally that I was no longer needed. It was my time with the Chargers that led to the opportunity with the Dolphins.

And it was while I was with the Chargers that I found linebacker coach Greg Manusky, who became more than a coach for me. He was a teacher and a mentor of the game in many respects. The man knew the game, having played it for nearly a decade as a linebacker himself and special-teams demon. What's more, he met me where I was—my knowledge and experience level. He was patient. Manusky excelled at identifying the exact thing I couldn't quite grasp and working with me until I got it. He was a great teacher because he gave grace to his players, demanding and understanding at the same time. And like I said, I had learned from my failure under Ryan that I needed to be more receptive to teaching. It was while playing under Manusky that I truly learned to embrace the linebacker position, and not only out of necessity. I learned the position because Manusky helped me understand the game of football at a level I never had before. Surprise, surprise—football is a more complex game than I ever imagined. But I learned it, and that was Manusky's gift to me.

Why do I embrace failure? Here's why: If not for my failure in Oakland, I would never have fought for a spot on the Chargers, which not only gave my career a second wind, but also introduced me to Manusky, whose teaching would prove invaluable to my second career. If not for Manusky, I wouldn't have the skills to talk football as an analyst. Learning what I did under Manusky gave me the confidence to enter that broadcasting booth and talk football to millions of strangers.

AKBAR GBAJABIAMILA

We learn to embrace failure because it's the only way we can improve. We sit in failure, because the pain is supposed to hurt. You must tear down those muscles to make them stronger.

A SEASON OF FAILURE

You already know that my first day on the set of *American Ninja Warrior* was a disaster. Well, so was my second day. And the third. In fact, my entire first season as cohost was probably the most painful showcase of failure I have ever experienced in my life. What made everything so much worse is that I was also experiencing depression in my personal life.

But to understand how and why I failed that first season—and how I eventually succeeded—we need to back up a bit. Earlier in my broadcasting career, I was calling college football games for CBS College Sports Network. I loved it. After doing grunt work (for free), I finally had this wonderful opportunity: a big stage, and a great place for me to hone my craft. For me it was the perfect stage on which to improve my skills. Having studied under Chargers linebacker coach Greg Manusky—and "study" is the right word for what I did—I was able to share my love, knowledge, and insight of the sport in a new way. I also really enjoyed being paid to talk football.

It was also at CBS College Sports Network where I worked under Ross Malloy. A producer at CBS, Malloy watched all of us in these smaller markets calling the games every weekend. He would take meticulous notes on each one of us, giving no-

152

nonsense critiques of our style, delivery, and commentary. After each game—and I do mean *immediately after each game*—the announcers and production team would get their report from Ross. It was just like Monday-morning film, where the team sat in a room and watched their failures—well, Ross's reports weren't that humiliating, but they served the same purpose. These reports could run several pages, and it's no wonder a lot of the guys hated them. They couldn't handle the criticism, which was a bit bizarre to me at the time. *Don't you want to get better?* I thought, whenever someone would blow up after reading Ross's notes.

I loved reading Ross's report on me after each game. I valued his direct criticism. His notes were harsh, but they were invaluable to someone who was looking to improve his talent, like I was. I read his notes meticulously and would go home and use them to study up for the next game, where I would try to implement his advice. Because that's how I saw it—he wasn't trying to hurt my feelings. He was telling me what I needed to hear, shorn of any fluff or honey. Maybe it was because of my experience as a player that Ross's criticisms didn't bother me like they did some of the other guys. And maybe it was one of those lessons I learned from my father, who would say: "Don't listen to the tone; listen to the words." I've learned that taking criticism is a skill, just like any other.

In any event, I never had a problem with taking criticism . . . until I started cohosting *American Ninja Warrior*. If my first day on the job was good for anything, it taught me that I needed to improve badly. I was ready to improve. "Tell me what to do!" I wanted to say. But I never received anything like I got from Ross Malloy. Have you ever been in a situation where you know you're failing but no one tells you that you are? It makes it worse, right? That's what was happening. I knew I wasn't giving the producers what they wanted—the sheer number of takes told me that—but they didn't hand me a report at the end of the day telling me what I needed to do.

I was also now in the entertainment world, not broadcasting. But it took me a while to understand the difference. In broadcasting, you're doing it live, on the spot, calling the play as it happens, offering a quick insight into why it happened, then waiting for the next play. Occasionally, during promo shoots and pregame material, you'll do "takes" that require a script, but they aren't a big part of the job, at least for the level I was at. You draw on your personality to make what you say sound exciting and interesting, but usually the camera isn't *on you* when you're saying it; it's on the field. *How* you say it doesn't matter as much as *what* you say.

Entertainment is different. *How* you say something, with the camera plastered to your face, is just as important—sometimes more—than what you say. Body language is how you speak. You bob your head at certain words; you raise your arm at certain points; and you read from a script word for word. Entertainment is all about taking direction. You're trying to recite a script from memory, use the proper body language and hand gestures, while someone is shouting at you to do it again, only do it *like this*. "Don't put your hand in your pocket," they would say. "And remember: big smile!" Smiling. Always about the smiling. I hated how everyone told me to smile.

I wasn't getting it, I knew I wasn't getting it, and no one really told me I wasn't getting it. But the constant attention and correction of the things I said, the way I spoke, started to bother me. When they said, "You can't speak like that, Akbar," what did they mean? That I sounded too black? I was very much aware that I was the first African American host amid a revolving door of hosts. I started to think all the criticism, the corrections, were racially motivated. At the time, I was battling severe insecurities over my inability to make the job work; then, my head went to these dark thoughts.

Calling the ninjas' runs was the one part of my new job that I felt comfortable doing. I drew on my experience as a broadcaster and added my own personality to the mix. I was being me, which is what I thought the producers wanted. But it wasn't. During voice-overs, I would get called out for saying things like "That boy good!" or "That's what sup!" or "My man just jumped!"

Um, excuse me, Mr. Gbajabiamila, but can you instead perhaps say: "That competitor is very good." Or maybe try: "That is what is up." But please don't say "My man." How about: "He just jumped." Okay?

I know now that it wasn't racially motivated, which I'll explain in a moment. But I wanted to give a sense of how failure nearly made me sabotage myself. I was on the precipice of a mental collapse and I was pushing myself over.

The worst was during voice-over work, when we would go into the studio to record segments. I was corrected on every little detail, every word, even every syllable. I would leave the sessions in tears. My first VO sessions would last four hours sometimes. (Now I get out of there in ninety minutes.) I was shocked at how dumb I seemed. I even went and got my IQ tested, just to make sure. Nope, I was perfectly fine. But you can see what sort of mental gymnastics I was playing on myself. I would take a bad moment and amplify it. I would take a piece of criticism and let it destroy my day. And when this happened day after day, my confidence shook, then was shattered. My life at work, my life at home—it all felt like it was crumbling down around me.

What bothered me most about all this wasn't that I was failing, but that I saw no way to succeed. Whenever I was in a position where my best wasn't good enough, I would use my time to reflect and work on my weaknesses. Being brutally honest with yourself is one of the rewards of failure. But when you fail because of who you are, then you can't improve on anything. I realize now that without knowing what I needed to do to get better, I was left to my own devices to try to figure it out. I was so lost in my own head that I turned on myself. I first thought I was failing because I was black, then I thought it was because I was dumb. How did I ever think I would make this work? What sort of delusions must I have had to think I was ready for this?

The irony is that somehow I did what they wanted me to do. We were living in my old childhood home in Crenshaw at the time, and I would work out at a local gym. After the season started to air, I ran into an old classmate of mine while I was working out.

"I can't tell the difference between you and the white guy," he said. That was a deep cut. What he was saying is that I had sold out to be where I was. I was dancing to their tune, hiding my background, where I came from, and who I was. Now, I don't think all that's true. What was true is that I wasn't being authentic. I started to mimic my cohost Matt Iseman's language and way of speaking. I thought that's what they wanted and so I looked to Matt to show me the way. But I hated burying my true self to mimic some polished, sanitized version of Akbar Gbajabiamila.

When taping had finished that first season in September, I had the same feeling as when I was under Rob Ryan's scheme in Oakland. I wasn't getting correction because they didn't care enough. They weren't screaming at me because they were already looking for a replacement. The writing was on the wall. I wouldn't be back for a second season. I accepted this to be true. I thanked all the crew and the production team for the opportunity. Then I left, wondering what I was going to do.

Toward the end of the year, I had a conversation with Brandon Riegg, who was a vice president of alternative programming at NBC. They were bringing me back. "You're capable of so much more," Brandon told me. His comment confirmed that I hadn't lived up to expectations, but it also said that maybe I hadn't been allowed to live up to them. The railings within which the producers had wanted me to operate had proved to take away the very thing that they had hired me to do. Instead of trying to manage me, make me be someone I wasn't, the new ethos was: "Let Akbar be Akbar."

It was only during the writing of this book that I finally sought the answers to all those questions I had during my first season. I called up our producer Kent Weed, who has worked on *ANW* since the beginning, and we talked it over. The first thing Kent reminded me of was that the show, prior to my arrival, had followed much more of a reality-TV format. When I came on board, the producers had decided to shift the format to be more like a sportscast. But they still retained the old production crew from the show's reality roots. That caused problems, most especially for me, because they thought they had to stage all my delivery.

So that explains part of it. I also asked Kent about my first-season struggles. "How come you guys didn't correct me?" He told me I had grammar issues, plain and simple. It wasn't that I sounded uneducated or "too black," but my grammar issues lessened the effect of what I was saying. They wanted the real Akbar, but back then, what I said didn't make much sense. That falls on me. Of course, part of the explanation was that they didn't want to "rattle the talent"—i.e., me. But it wasn't to save my precious ego (which was pretty much shattered anyway). As Kent explained it, they wanted my intensity, the feeling I bring to the show. They didn't want me to back down an inch from that. All the problems? They could fix that in postproduction. (Another difference between broadcasting and entertainment: postproduction is where the magic happens.)

Then Kent said: "Akbar, we give you all the credit: You worked on the things you needed to work on."

That felt great to hear, after so many years. My race had nothing to do with it; my intelligence had nothing to do with it. I was just inexperienced. I needed time to develop on my own. I was fortunate and blessed that they gave me that time to learn, to grow, to find my own voice.

I went into my second season determined to be me. And something happened when they gave me that freedom: I got better at those other things I was terrible at. I lost my feelings of inadequacy and I could suddenly take on those challenges without all that added pressure, like learning how to read a teleprompter well. The difference is that I am more conscious of what I say and how I say it. There's still a line of professionalism that one needs to walk, and I learned to walk it well. Today, when you see me screaming and shouting, you might think you see someone who is just letting it all hang out there. (True, in some cases.) The reality is that it's all very deliberate. I have been able to hone my craft and deliver the emotion with more rhythm.

And I can say that the Akbar you see on the screen is the real Akbar. When I'm losing my mind during a run, I'm in the moment. I'm cheering the way I wanted people to always cheer for me. I want to celebrate the ninjas—their courage, their strength, and their journeys. One of the greatest compliments I have ever received from my work on the show came from Jessie Graff, one of the greatest competitors the show has ever seen. She said, "Akbar, I never realized that a lot of the stuff I used to do was a big deal until I heard your excitement."

It took time to get to this point. It took practice. And, yes, it took me failing miserably at it my first time out. But I love my job. I would do it for free (almost). I have arrived at where I'm supposed to be. And I got here because I failed.

ONE OF THE "WORST" DRAFT PICKS EVER

Sometime around his second year in the NFL, my friend and former teammate Nnamdi Asomugha paid a visit to a woman who had watched him grow up. He called her "Granny," and she lived in East Oakland. When Nnamdi arrived, Granny couldn't wait to show him the front page of the sports section in the newspaper. She was always saving articles about him, so Nnamdi thought nothing of it. He looked down at the paper and saw a photograph of himself. Then he read the headline.

"I don't recall the exact words, but the gist is that it said: 'Worst Raiders Draft Pick Ever,'" Nnamdi says. "I realized then Granny had no idea what it said. She just saw my picture. She went back in the kitchen, and I pocketed the article. I left with it because I didn't want her to read it."

That's when Nnamdi stopped reading articles about himself.

I've known Nnamdi for almost twenty years. We first met in college at the All-Star East-West Shrine game and had hit it off. However, our friendship really started to grow when we were both rookies at the Raiders training camp in 2003. I was an undrafted free agent fighting tooth and nail for a roster spot; Nnamdi was a first-round draft pick out of the University of California, Berkeley. When you're chosen in the first round, the team is basically saying: *You're the future of the franchise at this position.* No pressure, right?

"I had no idea I was going to be a first-rounder," Nnamdi tells me. "I was as surprised as everyone else. Except everyone else was saying that the Raiders had just wasted a first-round pick."

The low expectations began for Nnamdi on Draft Day. Even the commissioner of the NFL, Paul Tagliabue, mispronounced his name in front of millions of viewers.

"On the TV, one of the sportscasters is saying, 'Don't tell me

I'm going to have to say this name every Sunday,'" Nnamdi recalls. "People just didn't know a lot about me. It's my first day in the NFL and I knew I had a lot to prove."

Which Nnamdi set out to do all through spring ball and into summer training camp. It was during our first practice in full pads that Nnamdi, who was transitioning from safety to cornerback, jumped to break up a pass and landed hard on his shoulder, dislocating it.

The injury was bad enough, but the blow to Nnamdi's confidence was almost worst.

"After the injury, I thought: 'It's over,'" he remembers. "Everyone was already skeptical, and now I'm injured. Now I'm missing my entire first training camp."

Teams don't usually cut first-rounders, even if they're injured. But that didn't do much for Nnamdi's confidence. Despite missing almost all of camp, Nnamdi made the team and spent most of the season hurt and working on special teams. During his entire first season Nnamdi remembers playing with the defense only a handful of times.

"I didn't know that a first-rounder was an investment and that they had at least a year to develop," says Nnamdi. "At the time, I felt like I would have a couple of seasons in the league and then that would be it."

The season ended and Nnamdi underwent surgery on his shoulder. He spent much of his off-season getting healthy, trying to learn the defense, and trying to understand his role on the team.

Looking back, Nnamdi says: "It was one of the greatest off-seasons known to man. Nonstop work. Work, work, work. I was working like an animal." The work paid off during spring practices, and the progress showed. "I was poised to dominate, and everyone saw it," he says.

Then camp started at the end of July and . . . something happened. He lost the progress. He lost his momentum and was playing like a rookie again. Most NFL veterans know that the few weeks between spring ball and training camp are very crucial for a football player. You have to keep up with your training and your conditioning so that you enter training camp better than you were a month before. Nnamdi did not. He made a "rookie" mistake. He would call his second-year training camp "the worst training camp in the history of training camps."

"The season starts, and I hadn't progressed at all," he says. "I probably even regressed a little, because I should've been at a certain level."

That's when the worst of the criticism started flying his way. That's when the label "worst draft pick ever" started being attached to Nnamdi. I asked him how he dealt with such pressure. I had been an undrafted free agent, which put pressure on me to make the team but at the same time relieved me of living up to anyone's expectations—other than my own. But to be on the other end like Nnamdi was, to have the expectation of greatness, and fail—I couldn't imagine how one handles that.

"Sports does an amazing thing to people," he says. "It teaches you how to get back up. There's no time to stay down. You still have to do it. I knew it wasn't working out, and I was frustrated. But the motion of getting up every day to practice and learn helped keep the momentum going."

Then, the turning point. As Nnamdi was leaving the weight room one day, he ran into one of his coaches.

The coach gave him this sort of despised look, then said: "I'd never have drafted you." Nnamdi didn't have much time to internalize the comment before another coach approached him. This time it was Rob Ryan, who must have heard what his fellow coach had said. Ryan stopped and said to Nnamdi, almost like it was just an afterthought: "You know what, Nam? Doesn't matter where you start; it matters where you finish."

"It was the greatest thing that could've happened to me," says Nnamdi, recalling the memory. "I don't know what would have happened if he didn't say that. But it gave me a second wind. It told me that I'm not done. That moment still lives with me."

A few weeks later during the season, Nnamdi was on the field against Kansas City, playing slot cornerback. It was one of the four snaps of the game that Nnamdi expected to play, and he was trying to make the most of his limited time.

The play started and "something happened."

"I thought, 'Wait, I've seen this formation on film, and I know what's about to happen.'" Nnamdi moved on the ball and hit the receiver so hard that he knocked him out of the game. The crowd went nuts.

"It was the first time the game slowed down for me," says Nnamdi. He ran back to the sidelines, where he met Rod Woodson, a Hall-of-Fame cornerback. "That was one of the best hits I've ever seen," Woodson said. "Keep it up."

Nnamdi kept it up. He became one of the best shutdown

corners of his generation. A perennial All-Pro and Pro Bowl cornerback. Fox Sports and *USA Today* named him a member of their NFL All-Decade Team for the 2000s.

At no time during those difficult moments did Nnamdi throw in the towel. But he also didn't ignore the ways he wasn't succeeding. He doesn't blame anyone for the struggles of his first two seasons. Yet he never stopped working. As he told me, he had to get up and do it, every day, every practice, every game. The game would eventually slow down, but it was by going through that motion of picking himself up off the floor that Nnamdi was able to step into his full potential.

In 2009, the *Oakland Tribune* ran an article in which Nnamdi was featured as one of the greatest Raiders of all time, with the caption "Best cover cornerback in the game."

From one of the "worst" draft picks to one of the best.

Nnamdi's story is one of success from failure. He didn't back away from failure and he certainly didn't dismiss it. He also didn't have to read the headlines; he knew the score. But he persevered. He accepted where he was failing and kept getting up every morning. Just as I had to go into the *American Ninja Warrior* studio despite my feelings of failure, so Nnamdi went out onto the field. And just as eventually everything clicked with me, so too did the game slow down for Nnamdi. Sitting in failure is painful; I don't pretend otherwise. But there's a purpose to that pain. If you feel it, if you learn from it, the pain will lead to success.

7

THE COST OF SACRIFICE

I thought I had made a nice little office. I had cleared out a whole portion of my childhood home to give myself some workspace. There were files over here, and stack upon stack of artificial turf over there. In truth, the place was a disaster, a complete mess. But it worked for me. I had a new job and I was going to make it work.

I had to make it work.

A few months prior, I had hit a crossroads in my life. It was 2011 and my broadcasting career wasn't paying the bills. When I had retired from the NFL, I had assumed I would rely on my NFL savings to get through the early rough patch. I had about $300,000 in savings when I left the NFL. In talking to others, I knew I would have to take low-paying gigs or gigs that didn't pay at all. I had done so, and I had accomplished a lot. To give some sense of my financial situation, here is what I was making in the years after I retired from the NFL.

2009: $26,000 (CBS College Sports Network)

2010: $28,500 (CBS College Sports Network)

2011: $35,000 (NBC Sports Network)

By 2011, I had a fraction of my NFL savings left. By this point, I was married with two kids and, like many, had taken some hits from the Great Recession. I had always been very careful with my spending, but the cost of supporting a family had depleted my savings quicker than I had anticipated. To make ends meet, we moved back into my childhood home in Crenshaw, because my father, who was suffering from Parkinson's disease, had gone to live with my brother in Green Bay.

I didn't think it was that bad, but my wife, Chrystal? She hated it. The schools in our neighborhood had low ratings, so we decided to enroll our kids in public schools out of our district that were nearly an hour away. So every day Chrystal would drive an hour to drop the kids off, an hour back, then an hour to pick them up, and an hour back. Four hours she was on the road. Combine that with the tough neighborhood surroundings, and you can only imagine my wife's resentment.

So I decided I had to join the job market, with barely any idea of what else I wanted—or could—do. I applied for jobs that required a communications degree and experience. I had done web design and development in college and fell back on that to bump up my résumé. Then I started to send it out. To be honest, I had hoped my name would give me a leg up. Even though I was never an NFL superstar—or a broadcasting star—I suspected someone would recognize me and give me a chance.

I was right—and I was wrong.

I'd get to these interviews and we'd start chatting.

"So I was looking over your résumé," the interviewer would begin, "and I'm a Raiders fan."

What would follow would be an extended conversation that reminded me of when fans would come to camp. We'd talk football the entire interview. I happily played along at first, naïvely believing I was getting somewhere. If they like Akbar the Football Player, then they'll like Akbar the Employee, right?

Nah, man.

After a few of these conversations that all went the same way, I started to wise up. When they would end the interview with "We'll get back to you," I knew it wasn't going to happen. I'll tell you what I felt, with the caveat that this might not have been how *they* saw it. I felt like I was nothing more than a football player to them—a jock. A guy on TV who knows how to use his body but can't be bothered to use his mind.

The whole process was demoralizing, as any job hunter would know. I felt like I was doing the right thing and still couldn't make it work. Those old feelings of not being good enough came swarming back. What would I do with my life?

Then through a friend, I learned about a sales opportunity at an artificial turf company. It wasn't in the communications field, but it was the one I got. I was excited. I had no concept of what it took to sell—and no passion for artificial turf either—but it was an opportunity. The pay? Base salary of $70,000 plus commission. Double what I had ever made in a year of doing broadcasting.

Besides, I would be selling to people who knew sports. I could talk "shop" and make a deal at the same time. And, truthfully, I loved that part of the job. Just meeting new people and sharing a good conversation. Of course, when they asked me about the specs of the turf, I stumbled. It's not that I didn't know about my product; it's that I had no passion for selling it. My ability to talk said nothing about my ability to sell.

The sad reality is that I wasn't a very good salesman. I remember preparing for a meeting the night before, frantically compiling sales packets and turf samples, making sure my polo shirt was clean and ironed, going over the details in my head—and stopping for a moment to think: *This is my life. I'm a salesman.*

I don't mean to knock sales, or any other profession. But in that moment in my childhood home, up to my neck in product I didn't care about, I suddenly saw a vision of my life that I had never intended. When had I ever wanted to be a salesman? When had I ever wanted to know artificial turf at the level that I needed to know it? When had I ever gotten a thrill out of working a lead toward buying something I was selling?

There are those for whom these are great things. They get a rush out of selling or have a passion for a product. Yet I realized that the *only* reason I was a salesman was because it provided a decent paycheck. I was in it for the money. Again, a lot of people love to make money. They get excited about the sale. I like money as much as the next person. I want to make money as much as the next person. But I don't live my life to make money. I make money to live my life.

I was grateful. I had a job; that is no small thing. A company had decided to give me a chance, a guy like me with zero sales experience. I worked extremely hard at it too. I hustled, following up on leads and burning the midnight oil to improve myself. I entertained clients, like when I took an athletic director to a Lakers game. My first sale came about six months in, and I got my first taste of what it's like to make commission. It was sweet. I started doing the math: If I make three sales, then that's an extra $18,000. The numbers began to add up in my head.

So *this* is what sales is all about. I can do this!

But I never got that far. Ten months into the job, not even a full year, I got the talking-to: "Akbar, this isn't working out. . . ." I was fired. They even sent a man to my father's house—my office—to take away all the company property, like the turf samples. The realization hit home. I had tried to do the "right" thing and I had failed. My faith in myself was shaken. I began to doubt whether I could make it in a "normal" job. But the deeper pain was this: What would I tell my wife? What would I do to support my family?

SACRIFICE: A DOUBLE-EDGED SWORD

We are told that we need to sacrifice for our dreams. We hear about stories of dirt-poor entrepreneurs working hard in their garages to build the next Amazon or Google. We hear about starving writers and artists who literally make themselves sick with devotion to their work. We see professional athletes sacrifice their bodies for their love of a game. We believe that, if we want to accomplish something truly great, then we too must sacrifice our fortunes, even our health, to make it happen.

And this is true, to some degree. Greatness doesn't just happen. It isn't easy. Unless we're talking about the lottery, no one finds themselves on a pile of riches without a trail of blood, sweat, and tears in their wake. But when does the cost become too great? Back in 2011, I had hit my limit. I had left the NFL in 2008 with a nice chunk of savings. Almost immediately after I retired, I called a friend and former teammate of mine from San Diego State, Andrew Kline, who also played in the NFL and transitioned to a successful career in the financial sector and nonprofits. I had always admired Andrew as a smart, savvy businessman, someone who had a direction for his life after football. And while I didn't want to go into the financial sector (too much math), I wanted to keep my options open. In fact, I wanted to do a lot. I was leaving the NFL with a bit of pent-up resentment and frustration, but thought that I would finally find my footing in my post-football career. I was energized and ambitious. I looked at some of my heroes, like Magic Johnson, and saw he had a hand in everything—entertainment, broadcasting, business, etc. The guy had a seemingly bottomless reserve of ideas. Magic was my model. I wanted it all.

Andrew's advice was blunt: "You need to pick one thing and focus on that."

But . . . but . . . but . . .

It was one of the best pieces of advice I'd ever received. My fear was that I would lose an opportunity by pursuing one goal. But when I got off the phone, I had to decide what I truly wanted to do. There was an incredible amount of pressure to "maintain the lifestyle" that the NFL had afforded me. But with the savings I had acquired I felt confident that I could advance my career first, then worry about money second. I realized that instead of missing out on opportunities, I was in a great position—a lucky position that few have in their life. So many must make that choice between money and passion. I could focus on my passion, then get to the point where I could make money. After some reflection, I decided I would throw myself into broadcasting and entertainment with everything I had.

In quick succession, however, I was married with a child on the way, and Chrystal had a child prior to our relationship. That alters the calculation somewhat. I went from one mouth to feed to four, and before I knew it that path toward my dream got a little bit rockier. When we're on our own, we can be brash and reckless. We can take risks and throw caution to the wind. We can travel and work without worrying that we're neglecting our duties back home. Duties? What were those before family?

What I'm saying is that it's easier to pursue greatness when our passion and ambition are our only concerns. Suddenly, I had other concerns. I acknowledged them, but I kept moving forward. The jobs were coming. I went from an unpaid internship in San Diego to CBS College Sports Network to NBC Sports Network, building a solid résumé of calling college football games. I traveled everywhere they sent me and did so willingly. I might have once naïvely thought I would have a career like Jerome Bettis, who went from an amazing NFL career as Pittsburgh's running back ("The Bus"!) to being hired by NBC to cohost *Football Night in America* the year he retired. But now I was a bit wiser. Yes, whatever they needed, I would do.

Which is how I found myself driving through cotton fields to go cover the Delta State vs. Shippensburg University game in Cleveland, Mississippi. I had flown into Memphis the night before, and early on game day, I jumped in my car, on the hunt for a barbershop to get a quick trim. (Full disclosure: I had developed some male-pattern baldness and was assiduous in keeping my dome cleanly shaved.) I usually traveled with clippers, but I had left them at home. As I was passing the fields of cotton, I pulled over to the side of the road on some random highway, the white puffy balls spreading out in all directions. I thought of the slaves under the sweltering sun picking the cotton and strayed out into the fields. I picked a few, only to realize that cotton is sharp. In any case, I got back in my car and headed out, finally coming across a barbershop.

The white barber took one look at me and said, in his thick Southern accent, "Sir, I don't cut your kind of hair."

The comment took me aback somewhat. I had experienced racism before, but it was a different, less overt form of racism. A racism of low expectations—of being a danger to white people, that kind of thing. Here was overt racism in my face: denial of service simply because of my skin color. But I was in a rush and didn't have time to get angry. I told the barber that I would pay to shave my own head. I just needed to use his clippers.

"Son, I don't cut your kind of hair," he repeated, angrier.

More shocked than offended, I looked at him. "I will pay you forty dollars to use your clippers." Who is so racist that he would refuse three times as much money as he would get for a normal haircut? And he didn't even have to touch me!

But the barber wouldn't budge. He directed me to a barbershop in the black neighborhood, calling at me as I walked out his door, "Don't step foot in my store again."

No problem there, homey. Those were the types of jobs I took, and was happy to do so. I recount this one bad experience, but I had far more positive ones. I love meeting new people in obscure corners of the country, learning about their lives, their troubles, their hopes, and what moves them. But as the years dragged on and my family grew, the novelty, the excitement, the sense of adventure of scraping by, following my dream, sticking it out—it all started to wane. The money that I thought was just around the corner never appeared. By 2011, I was down to $40,000 from my NFL savings. None of the jobs I had taken in broadcasting had paid that much a year.

I wasn't just running out of money. I was running out of time. How long could I continue pursuing this dream? What was the breaking point? Had I hit it?

When Chrystal and I got married in 2009, I asked her to quit her job. It was a hard choice for Chrystal to make. Working was part of her identity, something she had always done. She didn't really know what a stay-at-home mom did all day, and it took her a couple of years to find her new identity. Perhaps the transition would have been easier for her if I was more present as a father and husband, but I was jetting around the country, getting thrown out of barbershops in Mississippi, and would come home exhausted. I didn't realize it at the time, but as my struggles to make a career in broadcasting mounted, I poured more of myself into work and building my career than I did my family.

I didn't see the effect my career (or pursuit of my career) was having on her. As our savings began to shrink, my anxiety grew. I thought I was the only one who was concerned, but Chrystal felt it too. I thought I was making a brilliant money-saving move when I moved the family to Crenshaw, but my wife saw it as "hell." That's literally how she describes it today. When we pulled to the curb for the first time, we watched a couple of guys getting arrested. And because it was my childhood home, some of my siblings would walk in and out like they still lived there. It wasn't so bad when I was home, but sometimes I wasn't. I can only imagine that would have been challenging for my wife.

What hurt even more was the knowledge that my wife, whom I had told to quit her job when our daughter was born, had been making more money *then* than I was at that moment. You want to talk about feeling like a failure? I was supposed to have had a head start. I was a former NFL player! And yet here I was, moving my family back into my childhood home, while I flew off to cover another college football game for low pay.

You know, we can handle disappointing ourselves. We can fall back on the old slogans ("Get back on the horse!") and our faith, for I prayed heavily, asking God to lead my steps during this difficult moment in my career. We can tell ourselves that our hard work, our perseverance, our determination will pay off eventually. We have all the time in the world for ourselves. We can wait for the success to come.

What I couldn't handle was disappointing my family, especially my wife. I couldn't handle the thought of *letting others down*, while I galloped off every day in search of my dreams. My stature as a man was crumbling. Something had to give, and I knew with increasing clarity what it was. And still, I kept going.

Pride before the fall . . .

I was too prideful to accept the hard truth. My wife would find jobs and say, "I think you'd be good at this. . . ." *That? I'm not doing that!* "I think you should go on Monster.com . . ." she would say. *I ain't going on no Monster.com!* I would get angry. Couldn't she see what I was trying to do? Couldn't she support my dreams? Couldn't she see how close I was? I was destined for great things! Why couldn't she see that?

Why . . . ?

Because, I now realize, those who love us do so regardless of what we do in the world. They love us regardless of how the world sees us—or how we see ourselves. My wife and my children don't care about Akbar the Great Broadcaster. My wife wanted a husband who could provide; my children wanted a father who would be there. That's what they cared about. Looking back on this difficult time in our lives, Chrystal says that she just wanted me to feel better. She could see how unhappy I was even if I couldn't. When she tried to help me find other jobs, which I took as a hit to my pride, she was only trying to help me.

Why couldn't they see everything I was trying to do? Why couldn't they share my dreams?

Because they didn't love me for my dreams. They loved me.

Our dreams point us in the right direction. They give us purpose. They can be a vision from God to use the gifts He has given us toward His glory. For that reason, we should pursue them relentlessly and vigorously. We should sacrifice material things, even immaterial things, like moments with our families and loved ones. We know we must make a choice—an easy life or a hard life. We choose the hard life because we know that the realization of our dreams is one reason we are here on earth.

But it's not the only reason.

THE FINE LINE

There's not a person who has achieved their dreams who hasn't sacrificed something to do so. To this very day, I sacrifice time with my family to fly around the country doing my job. The sacrifice never ends. But I will say something that I doubt appears in books that talk about achieving your dreams: Sometimes the sacrifice is too great. Sometimes you must walk away.

I say this because when we sacrifice for our dreams, we're not the only ones who must sacrifice. We're asking those close to us to sacrifice as well. My wife sacrificed during those tough months in 2011. My children sacrificed time with their father. Because they love us, they will sacrifice. Because they love us, they will go on sacrificing even when they stop seeing a reason. Maybe they'll speak up, their voice like a terrible slap in the face back to reality, and we'll see just how much we're asking of them. More likely, by the time they speak up, they've been feeling that way for a long time—too long.

I saw my struggles as an investment—a necessary price to pay for something that will pay off in the long term. But my wife started to believe I was acting selfishly. The pursuit of dreams, of achieving greatness, is itself a very personal act. We do it to answer some need inside us or to fulfill our own idea of destiny. The rest of the world doesn't care about those things. Even if your dream has a philanthropic angle, the fact that *you* are the one who must do it and make it great carries a selfish motive. No president who was ever elected (or ever tried to get elected) did so without an underpinning of selfishness. We can call it ambition; we can say it's our calling—whatever the label, we are, at some level, doing it for ourselves.

But I hasten to add that doing something for yourself shouldn't be a bad thing, even if it is selfish. God gives us gifts to use to the best of our ability. He wants us to be great. Otherwise, He would have made all of us the same. What's more, He makes us work for it. He asks us to sacrifice for what we want in life. We wouldn't value the process or the journey, if He didn't. But most people in the world don't get to do what they want. Some because of their circumstances, others because it's just *too hard*.

But when we pursue our dreams without regard for others, then we've crossed a line. When we've lost sight of the other things in life that give us meaning, the gifts God has given us, then we have warped His purpose. We pursue greatness for His glory, but there is no glory to be found at the end of a path that is dark and isolated. I wouldn't want to be the Akbar who achieved all his professional dreams but left a trail of human wreckage—a neglected wife, forgotten kids, and a family who didn't recognize their own father. That Akbar might have made it on the big stage, but that Akbar would've lost everything else to get there.

I had to remember where my true purpose was—and is always: as a husband and father. God might have given me a talent for broadcasting, but He also gave me the gifts of a loving, beautiful wife and children. When we pursue our dreams, we ask them to sacrifice as much as we do. Sometimes more. I couldn't ignore their sacrifice. And that's when I stepped back and tried another road.

I can't say where the line is between sacrifice and selfishness. It's different for everyone. You probably can't say where yours is at this moment. But, believe me, it exists. Also believe me when I say that you will likely get very close to it during your journey. If it's a dream worth sacrificing for, then it's a dream that's going to ask you to make hard decisions. God gave you the dream to begin with, He gave you the vision, talent, and determination to go after it, but He also gave you the gifts that make achieving it worth the sacrifice.

Don't lose those gifts.

THE VIRTUE OF PATIENCE

I said previously that you might have to walk away from your dream. I didn't say you should give it up entirely. Only you know if the dream you're pursuing is one worth pursuing or one you should not be pursuing. You know your dream is worth pursuing if it aligns with your purpose. To find your purpose, it takes courage to be honest with yourself—and not fall for an idea of yourself. I might have had the dream to be a professional basketball player in high school. Through serious reflection, I had to accept that that dream was never going to happen. I could've sacrificed everything, given up everyone dear to me, and *still* I would never have been a professional basketball player. Fortunately, I learned that my dream was unrealistic at a young age, and I had to give it up.

But I never gave up on my dream of being in broadcasting or entertainment. I can't say for certain what would have happened had I turned out to be a good salesman. The money was certainly nice and perhaps I would've just slowly turned away from the camera. Even during those ten months when I was gainfully employed, I still went on auditions and even starred in a commercial (that never aired). When I was fired from the sales job, I had very little hope that I would be able to pick up my broadcasting career where I left it. I thought I would just fade away.

But God is good. Not a month later, I got a call from my agent, Mark Lepselter from Maxx Sports & Entertainment, asking me if I wanted to audition for a spot on an NFL Network show. I asked him what the show was about, and he said, "Fantasy football." Now, I understand there's probably the belief that all football players, current and former, are awesome at fantasy football. After all, we lived it; some of us even know the guys fantasy owners draft, analyze, and trade. But the truth is I had never played fantasy football. I didn't know anything about it. I followed football, college and the NFL, for professional reasons. I never knew when I would be called into a broadcast to give my two cents. But fantasy football is a different beast entirely. The performance of any one team is far less important than the performances and expectations of individual players. Even kickers! The focus is entirely different, which means that the knowledge required is entirely different. I didn't have that knowledge, but do you think I told my agent that? Heck, no. Man, I loved fantasy football! Yes, I wanted to do the audition!

Then I called my old football agent and friend, Bruce Tollner.

"Hey, Akbar, what's up?"

"Tell me everything you know about fantasy football," I said.

A laugh on the other end, then, "Swing by my office tomorrow. We'll take care of you."

So I showed up at Bruce's office the next day, as invited. He worked with a guy who knew a lot about fantasy football, and thus began my crash course on all things fantasy football. Here's how bad it was when I started. I could tell you the teams in the divisions I played for, which were all AFC West and East teams, because those are the teams you'd play twice a season, but I couldn't tell you any of the others. There are six other divisions! Not a clue. Which means that my "fantasy football training camp" started with the basics, then expanded from there. What's more, I was a defensive guy my whole life. I didn't know the depth of offensive players (like who was the number two wide receiver on the Chicago Bears) at all, yet which side of the ball does fantasy football focus on? The offense. I had to learn the quarterbacks, running backs, wide receivers, tight ends, and, yes, even kickers for all thirty-two teams!

I lived in that office every day for three weeks. Bruce's friend held mock drafts, quizzed me on players, and tested my knowledge of schedules—everything that even the worst player in your fantasy league knows. I was auditioning to be an expert. I was trying to be the guy who the best player in your league watches to find out what to do. But I'll say this: I felt alive again. I was happy to spend so many hours holed up in an office running through every conceivable angle of fantasy football, if it would help me get back to doing what I loved. My wife was surely happy to see me busy and not moping around the house, although she did reply to hearing about the audition with: "You're doing that again?"

Three weeks later I walked into the audition. I was as prepared as I could've been, given everything I had to learn in so short a time. The day was a whirlwind. Three or four of us would sit around a desk, cameras rolling, and a producer would shout out a topic. And we just dove in. They would switch up the talent, trying to find the right combination of personalities on set. Four hours later, I left the studio, exhausted and doubtful of my chances. It's the same feeling after taking a test that you crammed all night for. I was bound to mess up something, and I'm sure I did. A few weeks went by, then

I got the call from my agent: I was now a part of the NFL Network as a member of its most popular show, *Fantasy Live*.

Stepping away from your dream isn't the same as giving it up. In fact, it takes more courage to stay at it, even if you aren't actively pursuing it, than it does to just walk away. Why? Because it's like the half-finished home project that you pass every morning and every night. It sits there, undone, taunting you to find the time and energy to drive home the last nail. It would be so much easier to just toss the thing in the trash, never to see it—and thus, never to worry about it—again. Instead, you must look at it, even as you go about your regular life, feeling the sting of not having finished the job.

When things get hard, when the sacrifice becomes too great, we don't throw away our dreams. We just reassess and recalibrate. To do that requires a great store of patience. Assuming we're stepping back because of the cost of the sacrifice, and not because we're just lazy, then we can use that time away from the punishing pursuit to regather our strength. All else being equal, I would have preferred my broadcasting career had continued, without a pause, simply because it's what I enjoyed doing. I love it. To stop doing what you love in order to do what you must is a test of extreme patience. But I also know that my time away from my chosen career gave me the space to reconsider the direction of my life.

Is this what I wanted?

Is this what my family wants?

Is this what God wants for me?

Yes, yes, and yes. Then, when the time is right, go back at it, with a renewed heart, a fresh perspective, and even greater deter-

mination and courage than before. One of the hardest things to do in life—certainly in this modern, digital age—is wait. Everything in our society is all about Now! We want it Now! We need it Now! When we can't get it Now!, then we assume we aren't meant to have it. No, all it might mean is that you need to wait a bit. And waiting requires patience.

The NFL Network came at a moment for me when I needed it most—and not just for my career. Looking back, the job marked the turning point for me at home. I was able to finally reflect on how I could pursue my career ambitions while also being a better husband and father. This didn't mean that everything with my life or career would be rainbows and sunshine from then on, but I started to find that balance we so desperately need.

I was at the NFL Network less than a year before I auditioned for *Ninja Warrior*.

WHATEVER IT TAKES

If there's a competitor whose name has become synonymous with *American Ninja Warrior*, it is Brian Arnold. First appearing in Season 4, Brian has competed in seven straight seasons, never failing to make it to Stage 2. In his second season, Brian became the first American to reach the Flying Bar obstacle on Stage 3. By that point, Brian had quit his day job as the director of a nursing home to focus entirely on his ninja training.

"I quit my day job and wasn't going to waste this opportunity," Brian told me about his decision. "I was going to be the best ninja warrior of all time."

Being the best had been a motivation for Brian since he was a child. With five brothers (and one sister), Brian constantly found himself competing against his siblings. Whatever they did, he wanted to do. They started to do rock climbing, so Brian started to do rock climbing. One of them started playing chess, so Brian started playing chess. But he was never as good as they were. He was always second or third. But by never being number one, Brian learned something valuable.

"What I found is that I would keep trying," he says. "It didn't matter what I did; if I tried long enough I could get good at something."

Take chess.

"I was so bad at it at first," he says. "My goal was just to beat my oldest brother once. I remember playing him for months, until that one game that I won. It didn't matter that I lost a thousand games, I beat him once." But Brian didn't stop there. He continued with chess and is now rated an expert at the game.

But it was rock climbing that led Brian to *American Ninja Warrior*. "I remember watching the show and thinking that if I could get on, I would win." It was another challenge. Another way for Brian to be the best.

But Brian's extreme competitive drive does have a dark side to it. "When I do something, I'm all in," he explains. "I have to be the best when I do something. It can be very bad."

When Brian decided to quit his job and focus on ninja training entirely, he and his girlfriend had just had their first daughter. Brian convinced his then-girlfriend that he would split his time between training and being a stay-at-home father. But it didn't really work out like that.

"For me, it was an easy decision, but it was a very selfish one," he says. "My fiancée had to sacrifice, and I would be the one training. But that's what I wanted to do anyway, so to me it wasn't much of a sacrifice."

It was at the end of Season 5 that Brian became the last American standing. The decision to quit his job, the sacrifice his fiancée had made, had paid off. Brian was, at that moment, the best.

Only he didn't stop there.

"The process was working, and I was getting better, so why go back to work?" he remembers thinking. "Again, it was an easy decision, but we were sacrificing financially. My fiancée was very supportive and continued to work, and I know I couldn't have done it without her. There was no way."

In Season 6, Brian once again beat Stage 3, which convinced him to go another year. In Season 7, Brian didn't conquer Stage 3, but he did win the first season of *Team Ninja Warrior*. But by then, his motivation had changed.

"The show was getting harder and they found my weaknesses," he says. It was after his fall in Season 7 that Brian decided it was time to go back to work.

"I couldn't put my family through the sacrifices anymore," he says. "It's one thing to be selfish and sacrifice for yourself, it's another to sacrifice the well-being of your family."

Brian says he had to "satisfy those voices" in his head, the ones that constantly demanded excellence, greatness, from him with whatever he set his mind and body to do. After three seasons of focusing entirely on training, he felt the voices had been satisfied—or at least quieted. He returned to work, moving on from nursing homes to being an entrepreneur, learning how to combine his need to provide for a family with his passion. His company, called Ninja Nation, provides mobile obstacle courses for kids under twelve.

Of his years devoted to training, Brian says, "I think I was probably the worst fiancé and dad for a long time." He's still trying to be the best, only his focus has shifted. "Now I'm trying to be the best dad, the best provider—it's not about me anymore. But I still want to be the best."

It was Brian's decision to quit his full-time job that had fired my imagination. I wanted to dig deeper into the mind of someone whose competitive fire spurred him to make such a huge sacrifice. But when we spoke, I realized that the sacrifices he made to be the best at *American Ninja Warrior* were very similar to the sacrifices I—and my family—made so I could succeed at broadcasting. And just like me, Brian hit his limit. He found his own line between sacrifice and selfishness. He took a step back but ended up moving forward.

8

BURN YOUR CANDLE

My phone alarm wakes me at 4:00 a.m. With bleary eyes, I put on my workout clothes, hop in the car, and drive about an hour to meet my trainer. If I don't get my workout in now, I never will. At 7:00 a.m., I'm back in the car, on the Los Angeles freeway, slurping down my breakfast, headed back home to pick up my son, who has track practice near the University of Southern California. I wait in the parking lot for his practice to finish at 9:15 a.m, happy for the brief quiet moment. But I'm not resting; I'm studying the show notes for my tapings at the NFL Network later that day. If I don't get my studying in now, I never will. I'm back home at 10:00 a.m., when I can finally shower and get ready. I have a production meeting at the NFL Network at 11:30 a.m. Afterward, I find a corner in the building to study for another production meeting at 2:00 p.m. Then my day is consumed with taping. I stay at the office to prep for tomorrow's shows, finally getting back home at 10:00 p.m. I gobble up some dinner. If I don't eat dinner now, I never will. I finally fall into bed at 11:00 p.m, double-checking that my phone alarm is set for 4:00 a.m. Because I do it all again the next day, only I must squeeze in voice-over work for *American Ninja Warrior* somewhere in there.

Such was a normal day for me in the summer of 2018. And if it stayed "normal," then it would be manageable. But my days rarely stayed normal. During this same summer, I cohosted the Macy's Fourth of July fireworks show, I taped a new version of *American Ninja Warrior* for kids (called *American Ninja Warrior Junior*), and, oh yeah, I was writing this book. In an ideal world, I would be able to allot the same time and energy to all these pursuits, moving efficiently from one to the next, in a seamless course that starts in the morning and ends at night. But none of us lives in an ideal world, which means I'm usually behind on something or forgetting something else. Screwups happen. I think that my production meeting is at 8:00 a.m.; it's at 7:30 a.m. I sometimes neglect my email correspondence, to the point that one television executive blew up at me over it.

"Akbar, I'm going to tell you something no one else will," he said, seething. "You are the absolute worst at email!"

He was right. I find the email process to be overwhelming. Looking at my inbox on any given day gives me what I call e-anxiety. It's a never-ending ordeal that can easily gobble up hours of my day, and I've never properly put boundaries on it.

Meaning, I've never developed a system that allows me to tackle email so that I don't feel like I'm drowning in it.

We sometimes think that pursuing our dream means we are dedicated to a single goal: make the NFL, write a book, build a business, lose weight. *That's* what we're doing. And we want to think that in our pursuit of this single goal we'll be able to ignore the rest of the world. Except we can't ignore the rest of the world *right now*. We have too much on our plate. And so, we wait. We wait for our calendars to clear, our days to free up, and *our moment* to arrive.

There are no perfect moments. Or, at least, you shouldn't be waiting around for one to get going. Life isn't always played at 100 percent. Now, we should strive to simplify our lives. Don't waste time on stupid tasks—stop checking Facebook!—and understand that you'll need to give up your free time. We find the time to pursue our opportunities *while* we're living our lives, with all the responsibilities and tasks that take up our days. Finding that success we seek is what happens before or after your nine-to-five job and during those two-week vacations every year.

Speaking of vacations, I was on one in Europe not long ago, when I had to fly home to work. So I did. And when I finished, I jumped right on a plane and flew back to Europe to finish the vacation. I was exhausted, not so much from the traveling—although that was tiring enough—but from the continual tug and pull from work on one end and my "personal life" on the other. I still try to schedule time away from work, but, increasingly, I look at vacations as times when work piles up. When I get home,

I must wade through a mountain of work that I could've handled more efficiently had I never gone on vacation in the first place. Whatever R & R I might have obtained on the vacation itself immediately evaporates the moment I'm back home.

Life isn't easy, but a life lived with purpose gives us more clarity. It is in fact easier to manage life when we are full of purpose than to try to make sense of the random forces tugging and pushing us. To live intentionally, with direction, is better than to navigate life aimlessly. Since I was young, I have almost always had goals, which clarified my choices. Now I'm on a path that is focused on having an impact on people. What's more, I know I'm on the right path, as exhausting as it sometimes is, and that I am doing what God designed me for.

Since hosting *American Ninja Warrior*, I can't tell you how many fans I've met who have told me, "I think I could be a competitor."

"You should go for it," I reply.

But then they shrug and say, "I don't have the time."

Very few people can go after what they want without feeling the pinch in another part of their lives. We have bills to pay and families to support and love. We can't just ignore these things, not unless we want our lives to become much harder. To do this, we can't be doing that. It's a simple equation. We make the most of the time we have, and we make sure we find the time we need.

We could leave it at that. "Find the time!" But it's not that simple. Most of us don't know how to "find the time." It sounds nice, but how does that help the single mother of three kids who's struggling to start a business? How does "find the time" help the teenager who cares for his sick father to pursue his athletic dreams? To them, "find the time" is a meaningless phrase concocted by those who never had to make tough choices.

Sure, I'll find the time. . . . HOW?

The problem, of course, is that when we can't find the time, we get down on ourselves. We see others pursuing and achieving their dreams, and we believe it's because they were blessed with a discipline and determination beyond the average person. We all experience bouts of laziness—what's more, we usually know when we're in the middle of one of those bouts. The thought of doing anything productive just isn't in the cards that hour (or day). But even the most determined among us are prone to laziness. I had to learn how to "find the time" for the things I wanted. It wasn't just a matter of discipline. It was about how to focus, how to set boundaries, and how to make time work for me.

And it was about remembering something my father told me years ago.

MASTER OF THE CALENDAR

Most of my life I've had to juggle multiple pursuits. As a teenager, I was a student-athlete. Although sports were my primary passion, I was also a serious student, and not just because I had to be for my parents. I genuinely enjoyed school and strived to do well. But as an athlete whose practices often went well into the evening, I'd come home hungry and tired. I often didn't have the energy to turn my attention to homework and just wanted to fall into bed. When I would complain to my father that I had too much going on, he would say: "Burn your candle."

What did that mean?

In Nigeria, when my father was young, constant electricity was a luxury. The people had it, but they couldn't rely on it. A few hours here, a few hours there, then darkness. But life didn't stop when the electricity did. Work needed to get done; chores needed doing; people needed to live. Out goes the electricity, out come the candles. To do the things that needed to be done, even without electricity, you had to burn your candle.

That, at least, was the literal meaning. The figurative meaning is that we can't add hours to our day, but we can decide how to use them. We need to make choices about how we're going to spend the finite number of hours that are given to us. Sometimes we need to put more effort into this task, other times into that task. Sometimes I had to stay up late or get up early, "burning my candle" in the night.

In high school, I developed a schedule. I knew that I didn't have the energy to stay up late. I needed rest after practice. So I would go to bed at 9:00 p.m. and wake up at 3:00 a.m. to study for a couple of hours, then try to catch a little bit more sleep. In this way, I learned how to manipulate time. The hours were there; I just had to figure out how to use them best. I could have focused on athletics alone, as a lot of kids do, but that would have led to poor grades. Yes, I was tired often, but was I tired enough to give up on something? Basketball or football? Nope. Academics? Can't give up on that either. So it was up at 3:00 a.m. and manage. I burned my candle.

Oh, how I wish for those simpler years when I only had practice and homework. My life today is one of perpetual motion. But I wouldn't get half of it done if I didn't understand the value of time. It is one of the most valuable assets we own. And how we choose to spend our time has a profound effect on who we are and where we're going.

A while back I was a guest on NBC's *Little Big Shots*, hosted by the incredible Steve Harvey. Steve is seemingly everywhere: hosting *The Steve Harvey Show*, *Family Feud*, and a radio show, and not to mention all the books he's written. All this hustle has earned him (so far) six Daytime Emmy Awards and fourteen—*fourteen!*—NAACP Image Awards. Not bad for a guy who was homeless for three years for a stretch in the 1980s. Back then, Steve was a struggling comedian who lived gig to gig. As a 2013 *People* interview revealed:

"Though he'd stay in hotels when he landed a gig that would put him up, once he was done, 'I had nowhere to go,' he says, and began living out of his 1976 Ford Tempo, using an Igloo cooler in the back seat as a makeshift refrigerator, and washing up in hotel bathrooms, gas stations, or swimming pool showers."

Given my total shamelessness in approaching those I admire, after the taping I asked him if he had a few minutes to chat. Now, a guy like Steve Harvey doesn't "have a few minutes." But he gave me thirty, and I'll never forget it. I asked him how he does it all. He makes it look so easy. He told me he does three things: First, he wakes up every morning and drops to his knees to pray; second, he puts together a gratitude list to remind him what's truly important in life; last, he said he's "a master" of his calendar.

"I know what I'm doing now till next year, every hour," he told me.

Wow. It sounded so simple, almost too simple. And yet this is the formula by which Steve Harvey gets it all done. The genius is that it is so simple. But it is also high-level stuff. Let's break it down:

Pray: Remember who you serve.

Gratitude: Remember what you have.

Calendar: Remember what you're doing.

That's how Steve Harvey "burns his candle."

We don't need to have a schedule like Steve Harvey's to start mastering our calendar. The sooner we learn to set boundaries on our time, the sooner we start protecting our most valuable asset. Like any asset, we need to start seeing minutes, hours, and days as denominations of currency. In other words, how are you going to spend that time? Are you going to spend it on something useful or are you going to waste it on the trivial?

A 2017 study found that the average American checks their phone eighty times a day, or once every twelve minutes. I don't know about you, but I'm not getting eighty calls a day. But we all know why we're looking at our phones: we're *wasting* time. We're looking at our social media; we're texting; we're playing a game. We're in the grips of an epidemic of FOMO (fear of missing out). What's going on that we should know? Who's doing something that is interesting?

I would never do it, but just once I want to ask someone who tells me that they "don't have time" to train for *American Ninja Warrior*, "How many times a day do you check your phone?" What if, instead of checking it every twelve minutes, you check it every twenty-four? Then every forty-eight? Now you just manipulated time. Now you just *recovered* time that otherwise would have been wasted, gone, never to return. Because, let's face it, there's a countdown timer on all of us. We don't get those seconds, minutes, hours, days, months, or years back.

The sad reality of our modern age is that we have more opportunities than ever to waste our time. And, equally as sad, we are also busier than ever—at least we say we are. The very word "busy" seems to have become a mark of distinction. "How are you doing?" "Busy," we say. Everyone's busy, as if we're afraid to admit that we just spent an hour scrolling through Instagram. Busy is good. Busy is important. Busy is a badge of honor. But being "busy" distracts us from what matters. "Busy" covers up our fears and legitimizes our laziness. "Busy" is another form of denial—we cover up our lack of progress toward what truly matters to us. We can be busy on a stationary bike, but we still aren't moving.

We shouldn't be busy; we should be productive. I should check my email more; I should be more responsive than I am. I need to develop a system that lets me handle email as just another task on my schedule. So far, I haven't been terribly good at this, probably because email recognizes no boundaries. The minute you open your inbox, there it is. I shut it out to avoid it.

I consciously avoid looking at my phone. That way, I don't get addicted to checking the latest post on social media. And I don't get into the habit of measuring my worth by how "busy" I am. I measure it by whether I stayed on mission: Did I do what I had to do? Not just my work, but the stuff that matters to me—was I a good father today, a good husband, a good friend? Did I pray, did I do something toward my goals? Was I taking care of my health? I can't say yes to every one of these questions every day. When we burn our candle, we must choose where we're going to expend our energies. But by being a master of my calendar, I usually say yes to most of them. And if I can do that, then it was a good, productive day.

We become masters of our calendar because we need to regain control of the time that is given to us. We start simple: just planning our coming week, setting aside a few hours toward our goal somewhere in those seven days. Then we move on to a day, carving out those twenty-four hours. One of the good things about the modern digital age is that we have no excuse for not keeping a calendar. Click, type, press enter. There, it's in our calendar. We also have no excuse for forgetting what's in our calendar. That phone we check eighty times a day has a buzzer, dozens of them.

We master our calendar, we set boundaries on our time, so that we can maximize living out our purpose, the plan God has for us. That's how we can burn our candle.

LIVE INTENTIONALLY

In high school I started to notice that I wasn't the best test taker. What I mean is that the format of the test—answer so many questions in a specific amount of time—didn't seem to fit how my brain worked. I studied hard and I knew the material, but come test day, when the clock started ticking down, when the other students would finish, I would get agitated. Then I'd panic. My reaction to this was very typical of me: I'd just work harder. Study harder. Ask more questions. Concentrate harder. And yet, it didn't come together on test day.

When I got to college, my problem only worsened. Students would be leaving, and I wasn't halfway through the test. It didn't matter how hard I studied, and that bothered me. Was I just dumb? How come all the other students could do it, but I couldn't? Fortunately, during one of the communications courses I took, my professor, Dr. Peter Andersen, noticed my test-taking problem and asked me about it. I would spend a lot of time with this professor after class, working on the subject material. He gave me all the time I needed and stayed with me until I got it. Which is why my test performance frustrated him as much as me. He *knew* I had it, so why wasn't it showing up on the test? Then one day he asked me:

"Have you ever been tested for a learning disability?"

I hadn't. But with his encouragement, I got tested and it turned out that I had a processing disorder, which means my brain works differently than most. More practically, it explains why I struggle with the traditional test format. I should've been happy that I had finally pinpointed the problem, but I was embarrassed. Something was wrong with me! It wounded my pride. The doctors mentioned medication could help, but I refused. And really, I refused because I could hear my father's voice in the back of my head: "You work through it! You got to be tough!" Taking medication would only confirm that I had a "problem," and I didn't want that. Fortunately, I called Melinda McMullen, my mentor and friend since I was in high school, who has worked at some pretty large companies. She told me that a lot of people she worked with—very senior, high-level executives—had the same problem. "You're not the only one, Akbar," she said. That helped tremendously. I could accept what I had wasn't anything to be ashamed of—I wasn't responsible—but I could choose what to do about it.

My processing disorder allowed me to take tests at the Student Disability Center, where I also got extra time. These changes made all the difference in the world. I could focus on the material, not on the time. Just as important, I didn't have all those panicky negative reactions when the other students finished before me. They didn't finish early because they studied harder or knew the material better. They just didn't have a processing disorder. So instead of *reacting* during my tests, I could approach the test the way I was meant to: as an evaluation of knowledge and critical thinking, not how quickly I could finish.

I mention this because when we talk about mastering our calendars, we're talking about making time work for us. Before

I knew I had a processing disorder, during a test time worked against me. I was jumping from one question to the next, trying to find the one I knew immediately, hoping I would have enough time to get back to the ones I didn't. It was a reactive exercise. I wasn't in command. Time was manipulating me. But once I could remove time from the test, I was back in control. I didn't have an infinite amount of time to finish, but I wasn't reacting; I was thinking. I was letting my brain figure out the problem, not react to the ticking clock.

To live reactively is a terrible thing. Reactive living is thoughtless living. It's a matter of responding to stimuli. Time is running out. Gotta do this! Gotta do that! When I was taking tests, my brain wasn't thinking about the problem or the best answer; it was just trying to finish. No wonder I got agitated. No wonder I panicked.

This is why procrastination is such a bad affliction. We wait, we wait, we wait some more, then, when time is running out, we rush and hurry. Maybe we get it done in time; maybe we don't. Regardless, we haven't done our best work. All we did was finish. Finishing something isn't the same as completing it. Maybe I "finish" my studying for my taping in an hour. But if I rush, I don't absorb the information.

As an athlete, procrastination will cost you and your team. You learn quickly that you can't procrastinate in sports because everything in athletics takes a long time to complete. You can't procrastinate on your lifting, then "cram" the week before. The body doesn't work like that. It needs time to build that muscle.

It's the same for learning your steps, moves, and techniques. You can't ignore these fundamentals in the vain hope that you'll train your mind and body the night before the game.

But procrastination is only part of the problem with living life reactively. There's no intent in reactions; it's an instinctual response to something being done to you. Something happens, then the reaction. When we're reacting, we're not in control. A life without intention is one that will float whichever way the wind blows. We need money, so we get a job. We need more money, so we get a bigger job. No thought is given as to whether it's the *right* job; the job itself is nothing more than a reaction to a stimulus— the need for money.

In some ways, my decision to get a job selling turf was an example of living reactively. Never once in my thirtysomething years of being on this planet had I ever said I wanted to sell or be in the turf business. But someone offered me a job, then bam! I was in the business of selling turf. I was going to be the best turf salesman in the world. I was offered something, and my reaction was to take it. My next reaction was to be great at it. Yet deep down, I probably knew that I wouldn't last. But I didn't want to believe that I was taking a job just to make money. I wanted to believe I was doing the right thing.

So is it any wonder that I wasn't happy selling turf? Is it any wonder that I got fired?

To live intentionally is to know where you're going strategically. It's to know *how* to spend those hours we might recapture through mastering our calendar. It's stopping pursuits and activi-

ties that don't move us any closer to that goal—and here, I don
just mean our dreams. I mean the things that we know matter t
us: our family, our faith, our friends, our health. We live inten
tionally so that we can maximize our time doing these things th
matter. We live intentionally because it allows us to go to bed ea
night fulfilled and wake up each morning excited. Why? Becau
our lives are aligned with our purpose. We are living as God war
us to live—productively and for His glory.

The most successful teams in the NFL aren't accidental abo
winning. They have a system in place that focuses all time a
effort toward a single goal. As individuals, we need to be just
deliberate with our lives. We need to develop a tactical syst
that moves us forward, a plan to get us from point A to po
B. This is why I'm so self-conscious and protective of my o
boundaries—the blocks of time I have scheduled during whic
am focused on a single task. Other tasks and people may dema
my time (and sometimes I must bow to their demands), but I
everything in its place. Right now, I'm working on this. The
will work on this. Methodically checking off the blocks of ti
focused on the task at hand, and not being pulled in multi
directions.

As always, easier said than done, especially when life in
venes. As a husband and father my first priority is to my fam
I schedule time with them—my most valuable block of ti
in the day, in fact—but I also have to be willing to break
calendar for their benefit. I fall back on my own childhood
this lesson, as does Chrystal, who was raised by a single mot

We must provide for our kids—that's one of the greatest lessons we both learned from our parents. But we also learned how important it is to be present in our children's lives. My parents did their best, but they often overlooked things that were important to me, like my games. Chrystal's mother was often working and rarely available when Chrystal needed her. Kids go through a lot of drama and pain growing up. As parents, we need to be there for them when it happens. Chrystal says her mother often wasn't. We take these childhood experiences and use them to guide us on how to raise our kids. We might not make every game, we might not be there at the exact moment they need us, but we try. We do our best, remembering that the most important part of our day is the time we spend together as a family.

We master our calendar so that we can manipulate time; we manipulate time so that we can start living intentionally, knowing where we want to go. Next, we find our direction, our bearing, when our vision is aligned with our core values.

FINDING OUR VISION

Around the year 2000, I was in college, playing football, but also going through a moment of discovery, as I mentioned in chapter 4. I had encountered Pastor Miles McPherson, who opened my eyes to the love of Christ. What I haven't talked about is the moment I decided to live for Jesus Christ. And frankly, I was a

little embarrassed by how it all happened. But I've since come to believe that moments like mine aren't all that unusual, and sometimes all we need to hear from others before we accept our own moments.

My moment started when I was in my apartment watching the movie *Men of Honor*. (Like I said, it's a bit embarrassing.) The movie stars Cuba Gooding Jr., who plays a master diver for the U.S. Navy. I started to doze during the movie and began to dream. I dreamed I was in a scene of the movie where Gooding's character was underwater trying to fix a part of a ship when he gets stuck. The drama kicks in as Gooding's oxygen levels start to get dangerously low.

There's a rational explanation for why I had this dream: I too felt stuck, underwater, unable to complete my task, and like time was running out. I had been searching for the meaning in my life but was unable to commit to it. I saw the power of Christ throughout my life, in the way His grace worked, not just on me, but on those I loved. I knew Christ was the answer, and yet, I hadn't given my life to Him.

I hadn't realized how much my soul was struggling to find its purpose. Not until I had this dream, and it was during it, stuck, underwater, gasping for air, that I heard a voice: "If you don't give your life to Christ, you're going to Hell." I woke up immediately. I was a bit disoriented, but mostly confused.

What was that? *Who* was that?

The next day, I had the same dream and I heard the same voice: "If you don't give your life to Christ, you're going to Hell."

Now I was starting to get worried. What was happening? It was a movie!

On the third day, the dream returned. "If you don't give yourself to Christ, you're going to Hell."

That's when I stopped trying to rationalize and started to understand. God works in mysterious ways, and it doesn't matter if He latches onto a scene from a movie to make us hear Him. I was underwater. I was trying to fix something, but I was running out of time. What was I trying to fix? Me? I can't say, but the dream represented where I was at that moment in my life. I was lost. I was struggling.

But with Christ, I don't need to struggle anymore. Whatever I was trying to fix, He heals. I wasn't gasping for air; I was gasping for His presence. This was the moment that I found the vision for my life that has guided me ever since, for this was the moment—over the course of three days—that I turned my life over to Jesus Christ. I don't need to struggle anymore because He is my Light. He shows me the way.

We often talk about discipline and motivation as if these are independent things. If only we had more motivation, more discipline, *then* we would get stuff done, be able to achieve our dreams. So we try to manufacture some. We put on our favorite running song or we fire up our favorite movie, and we feel that jolt. Yes, now I'm going to start! I'm going to do this every day. We set aside an hour every day for our run. Usually, we would take that extra hour to sleep, but not anymore. Now we're going to master our calendar. Now we're going to stop wasting time!

But what always happens? The song ends and the next day comes. You put the song back on, but the jolt isn't quite as strong. We don't feel quite the same rush as before. Maybe it's enough to get us out the door that day, but already we feel our motivation and discipline waning. Eventually, we're tapped out. The song doesn't work anymore. Our alarm wakes us up, but we'd rather sleep. A day may come when we feel that panic—gotta get it done!—and we rush out the door, but these moments become the exception. We're back to where we started, and all because we didn't have any motivation or discipline.

No, it's more than that. What we lack is vision. Vision gives us direction. When we have a vision, we will find our motivation and discipline. Inspiration is like the key in the ignition—it starts the car. But perspiration gets the car to the destination. Everything I am and everything I do or try to do is because of my faith in Jesus Christ. He is my strength. He gets me up at 4:00 a.m. and pushes me all day before I collapse in my bed at night. He is both the flame of my ambition and my check. He uses me for His glory, but also never lets me lose sight of what already makes me great: my wife, my children, my friends.

I've always been a hard worker. Getting in shape, exercising, leading a healthy lifestyle—these have never been my weaknesses. I still draw on my faith for those days when my own will just isn't strong enough, but I know I was blessed with a discipline and work ethic that comes from my parents and God. But everyone has their weaknesses, and I have many. One that has been a constant theme throughout this book is my own self-doubt and negativity. I'm incredibly hard on myself, and this self-criticism can lead to periods of low confidence. My recourse has always been to work harder, and sometimes that is enough. But sometimes, particularly during my broadcast career, it's not enough.

God got me through that first season of *American Ninja Warrior*. My faith that He wouldn't lead me astray kept my head above water. He had planted in me this desire to pursue a career in broadcasting and entertainment. I had achieved enough by then to know I was on the right course. God got me up and into work every morning when I was convinced I was about to be fired. He was my strength when it was hard to find any on my own.

This is why vision is different than dreams. We often use the two words synonymously, but I look at it this way:

Dreams are where you want to go. Vision is why you want to get there. On their own, dreams can't generate enough discipline and motivation. Everyone has dreams; few realize them. The reason why is because a dream without a vision is just a wish. We might have dreams of being millionaires, but if that doesn't happen we'll probably be fine. Nothing is going to happen to us if we don't pursue that dream. We might as well wish to win the lottery.

Now, if you want to be a millionaire because a million dollars will help support your sick child or parent, or provide the capital to start your business—well, now that dream has a vision attached. There's a *reason* you're going after that dream. There are stakes involved. If you fail to achieve this dream, you aren't the only one affected. If there are stakes attached to your dreams, then *that's* motivation. That will lead to discipline.

I wanted to make the NFL for many reasons. But the primary reason is it was the realization of years of work and effort. I saw the NFL as an opportunity not just to make money, but to open doors for me that would otherwise remain closed. I loved the game, but the NFL was so much more to me than playing. The great fear I had, particularly after my Achilles tendon injury, was that I would have to go back to the hood and just be one of the guys who never made it out. Worse, I would've been one of those who *should* have made it out.

That was my motivation. There were stakes. I might still have failed to make the NFL, just as I might have failed in entertainment and broadcasting, but I wasn't going to be the cause of the failure. I wouldn't have to look back and say, "I could've done more."

Having a vision has helped me look at the dreams I've had and choices I've made in my life and know that I'm doing what I should be doing. I look back on the child who loved to watch Oprah Winfrey, who watched videos of the power of words being uttered by Muhammad Ali or Malcolm X, and I can say that those were signs. And when I went through my moments of doubt and periods of failure, when I wondered if I had been crazy to think I could do this, I relied on my vision, and God's design for my life, to pull me through.

I'm not crazy. I'm good enough.

And like the second wind that hits a runner at just the right moment, I am refreshed. I am rejuvenated and inspired to go after it another day. Forget the silly songs that get your heart pumping. We need something more to make us work day after day, week after week, and year after year, to live a life of purpose, of meaning, and by God's design. We cannot create the level of motivation that is required to find greatness through artificial means. Sure, fire up that song, watch that movie, but know that true motivation and discipline come from a deeper source. To be truly inspired is to strive for the benefit of something greater than you.

Finding that vision for ourselves is an essential part of our journey toward greatness, far surpassing how we organize our calendar. Because it doesn't matter what you put on your calendar if you don't continue to have the motivation to do it. It doesn't matter if you strive to live your life intentionally, with a direction in mind, if you don't know why you're going there.

We all want to be great. We all want to be ninjas. But we first must learn why.

RUN TOWARD SOMETHING

I first met Melinda McMullen when I was in the tenth grade, but she has been in my life ever since. Our relationship has evolved over time, from Food from the 'Hood adviser to mentor and now to a good friend. So it was only natural that I reached out to her as I began working on this book.

Melinda spent her career in leadership roles at some of the world's largest PR firms and at big corporations like IBM and JPMorgan Chase. But ask her to name the toughest job she ever had or the one she cared about most passionately and she will tell you it was Food from the 'Hood, the high-school-based student-owned company in South Central Los Angeles where we met.

Melinda helped plant the original seeds for Food from the 'Hood. The company grew out of the Los Angeles riots, which began on April 29, 1992, and continued for six days. Most of us kids sat prisoner in our homes watching as our community gave way to fires, looting, and horrific violence.

"I saw Los Angeles, a community that I cared deeply about, go up in flames," she says. "Many of us were asking why people would riot and burn property in their own community, but one of the cleanup volunteers made an important point. He said that the people who took part in the looting and burning may live in the inner city, but they didn't own anything there. I realized he was right. Most of the businesses in South Central Los Angeles were owned by outsiders."

In that moment, Melinda decided that business ownership should be a focus in the inner city. After dozens of phone calls, she connected with a science teacher at Crenshaw High School who also wanted to do something. When the school year began five months later, they brought together a group of high school students who created the business that became Food from the 'Hood.

As with the ninjas on the show, Melinda is passionately committed to everything she does, and I can tell you from experience that it's infectious. As I look back at what we accomplished at Food from the 'Hood—a bunch of high school students getting a salad dressing into more than two thousand grocery stores in less than two years—I am still amazed, but Melinda was relentless. She would not give up. I asked her how it all came together.

First, she told me, she never let go of the goal: to help a group of high school students start a business—something they could own and be proud of. She pointed out, however, that she was willing to let the idea evolve over time. When the original business (organic farming) didn't prove financially successful, she worked with us to rethink our plan, which grew into the salad dressing business. In other words, the goal remained the same, but she allowed the strategic path to achieving our goal to evolve.

Second, Melinda said that throughout her career she had tried to work with and learn from people who were smarter than she was. She pointed to Norris Bernstein, a highly successful salad dressing entrepreneur, as a key factor in Food from the 'Hood's success. Like Melinda, Norris didn't have much in common with a group of inner-city teens—he was retired, white, and always wore a suit—but Norris treated us as peers and with respect. He taught us about the salad dressing business and gave us some amazing advice, but he also made it clear that Food from the 'Hood was *our* business and that *we* were in charge.

Melinda's last bit of advice really struck home with me. She said she always tries to run *toward* things. "I've had experience running away from things and it's easy for me to lose my way," she says. "But when I run toward something—preferably something I'm passionate about—it's easier to map the route, create the plan, and stay motivated even when things get tough."

"I'm not good at perfunctory work," she says. "I'm not good at average. For me, it all comes down to having a big, tough goal and answering one question: Why is it important to succeed? If I take the time to focus on articulating the goal and answering that question, very little can get in my way."

"Some people think that finding your passion is like finding a soul mate—that there's only one thing out there—but I don't believe we are born to do just one thing. Life is long and circumstances change. For me, the trick is discovering the passion in whatever it is I'm doing."

Melinda said that regardless of where she worked, whether at Food from the 'Hood or in corporate America, her overarching goal was to have a positive impact on the company and on those around her. "That fairly simple philosophy served me well," she said. "Professionally, I did well, but perhaps more important was the fact that I was very happy."

Melinda says people have asked her over the years if she would like to do anything like Food from the 'Hood again, but she says once was enough. She enjoys tackling difficult challenges, but once they are accomplished, she believes in moving on to something else. The challenge, she told me, has been to continually be on the lookout for new things to do, whether for pay or not, that bring her life meaning.

Melinda retired six years ago, but she said she still wakes up every day with the goal of having a positive impact on the world around her. Today she lives on a farm in rural Michigan, where she said she takes joy in helping friends and neighbors, staying in touch with old friends, and spending time working with nonprofits she cares about.

"I'm at a stage in my life where I'm no longer working for a living, but I still try to wake up in the morning with a goal to run toward. The nature of my goals may have changed a bit, but the act of running toward something has never wavered. I've found that it's what fuels my happiness and brings my life meaning."

I have been learning from Melinda since I was teenager. She taught me so much about business and finances, about how to create and own something that is uniquely yours. But after speaking to her, I also see why Melinda was such an avid and inspiring teacher and mentor. She helped because that's what fueled her passion. As she does with everything she touches, Melinda found purpose with the students of Food from the 'Hood. But she also found purpose in her other jobs too. Melinda is successful because she was able to find her purpose, and it was her purpose that ignited her passion.

9

WHO DO YOU FIGHT FOR?

Growing up, my favorite athlete was Muhammad Ali. He still is in many ways. His dominance in the ring, swagger, and sense of justice made Ali into something that no one else has ever matched. He was more than a role model for a kid from the hood. He was like a superhero to me, a real-life Superman who didn't seem to be a part of this world. And yet he was just a man, a fact made terribly clear when this larger-than-life giant became riddled with Parkinson's disease. I know I wasn't the only one who cried during the opening ceremony of the 1996 Summer Olympics in Atlanta when Ali, shaking, proudly held aloft the torch, revealing a glimpse of the power and presence of his younger self.

And one of the greatest moments in my life was when I met Ali. The year was 2001 and I was in college. The Will Smith movie *Ali* had just come out and as chance would have it, my older brother Foley worked for Interscope Records, which did the music for the film. Foley was able to get me tickets to the premiere at the Palm Casino in LA, which also gave us access to what was essentially backstage. My brother, whose career allowed him to mingle with big music stars like Tupac and Dr. Dre, and knowing how much I idolized Ali, said to me before we walked in the room, "Act like you've been here before."

No problem.

Then we entered the room, and there were Jamie Foxx and the man himself, Muhammad Ali, who had brought his daughters to the film premiere. It was like I was in a dream. I don't want to take anything away from the star power of Foxx, but no one—and I mean, no one—overshadows Muhammad Ali. I felt my hand inch toward the camera in my pocket, already forgetting Foley's warning to behave myself. Then Ali sees me. *Muhammad Ali is looking at me*, I hear my mind scream. The champ points a trembling finger at me, motioning for me to come over. My heart is pounding through my chest, and my palms are slick with sweat.

I walk over to him, and he's telling jokes. I don't understand much of what he says, but his daughter Laila is translating for him. I'm in the presence of greatness, and I'm so overwhelmed that I can't think straight. Ali then turns to me and asks me my name. I tell him Akbar, and immediately he says, "Allahu Akbar," meaning "God is great" in Arabic. I want to ask him for an autograph, but, remembering Foley's warning and gripped with my own fear, I never do. The moment passes into memory.

But you can believe I told the story later to my teammates at San Diego State. The only problem was that they didn't believe me. "You ain't never met Muhammad Ali!" they said. Without proof, not so much as a picture, it was just my word—and Ali's stature was so immense back then that I might as well have told my friends I had met Dr. Martin Luther King, Jr.

A few days before Christmas Day 2001, when *Ali* was released in theaters, a letter came to me in the mail. Inside was a 22-by-26-inch framed and autographed photo of Muhammad Ali, dated December 8, 2001, with the greeting "To Akbar." It remains the greatest Christmas gift I have ever received, and not because it was an autographed picture of Ali; the gift is that Muhammad Ali thought enough of me to remember me.

Yet meeting Ali was more than the realization of a childhood dream. About a year earlier, my father was diagnosed with Parkinson's disease. When I saw Ali, surrounded by his entourage, the focus of a thousand, I saw my father's future: the trembling, the slurred speech, the physical diminishment of a man whose physical presence had captivated the world. And that's one thing Ali and my father shared: an overpowering physical presence, one that was going to shrivel because of a tragic disease that didn't care how big, how powerful, or how famous its victim was. The decline was inevitable.

But what if it wasn't inevitable? What if it was preventable?

We can ask these questions not because of some false hope for a miracle. We can ask them because thousands of people, this very moment, are working tirelessly on a cure for Parkinson's. And it's been one of the defining visions of my life to help them.

A SIMPLE CALCULATION

When I was nine years old, my father took me to the store to buy hundreds of donuts. We then drove to Skid Row in downtown LA. We got out of the car and started to hand out the donuts to the homeless and other unfortunates who called this forsaken part of the city home. Most people who live in LA prefer to forget that a place like Skid Row exists. They would rather forget that its people who line the streets and alleys are people at all. They're shadows, to disappear in the bright California sunlight. In the darkness, they are ghosts, to be avoided at all costs. Standing there with my father, I feared the people who shuffled up to us, overjoyed to have a little something sweet to eat. I didn't understand why we were there, and what my father was doing. I mean, I knew we were helping these people, but I didn't understand why.

After all, my father just spent a lot of money on donuts. That's money that could've gone for something for us, his family! We needed things. We weren't rich. In fact, I'm certain that my parents qualified for welfare support, yet they never took a dime from the government. But to give someone else charity? I didn't understand.

I didn't need to understand. I saw it, and I watched my father happily spend the money he had earned, to make someone else's life just a bit easier. He had more, they had less. That was the simple calculation. He didn't expect accolades. He didn't call a reporter or television crew to watch him hand out donuts. After all, who would care about a Nigerian plumber from Crenshaw? In fact, until this very moment, with you reading this, I doubt anyone other than my family knew what my father had done to help the homeless on Skid Row.

I mean, other than those he helped. And that's the point. We shouldn't do nice things for others because we want recognition. We shouldn't do it because we are famous and have a platform and that's what we "should" do. We shouldn't do it because we've accomplished our own life goals and are *now* ready to give a little back. We hand out donuts to the homeless on Skid Row because they appreciate it. We have more, they have less. A simple calculation.

My father's sense of charity extended to his customers as well. I remember going out on call with him one day. It was one of those emergency, last-minute kinds of jobs, and in the plumbing world, that could mean a real bad day for the customer. My father fixes the problem and is ready to settle the bill. Except the customer can't pay. He doesn't have the money with him. My father waves it off. "That's fine," he says. I'm shocked. I understand helping those less fortunate, but this wasn't charity. This was a job, a free exchange of goods and services. The service was rendered, now comes the exchange. But that's not how my father saw it. The man needed help, and my father had the ability to help him. Again, a simple calculation.

Of course, my father couldn't do that for all his customers. I don't know how often he waived a fee, but I know that I didn't witness the only example. Nor was the day he took me to Skid

Row the only time he gave food to the needy. To say that this was who he was is a bit unsatisfying. *Why* he did it comes down to many factors, not least of which is that's what his Muslim faith asked of him. But I also know that he found joy in being of service to others, whether they were homeless or his customers. He lived by example and raised his children with the same appreciation for service, not because it was a duty, but because he knew that one day we would receive the same joy.

Sometimes my father's lesson would come by way of example; other times he would be more explicit. He once told me, when I was a teenager, that my height—I was well above six feet tall in high school—carried with it an obligation. How did my height, which I had no say in, give me an obligation?

"Because people will always notice you first," he said. "They will expect you to help them."

What he meant was that height is a privilege. Sure, it brings its own drawbacks, but overall, my height gives me advantages that most others don't have. Someone needs to reach an item on the top shelf. I can help. Someone needs to change a ceiling light bulb. I can help. Even my size and strength, a lot of which I was born with, give me an obligation to help those who are weaker. A friend needs help moving. I can help.

After all, my last name—Gbajabiamila—means "big man, come save me." Heck, when it's your name, you gotta help!

Yet all of us have something that others don't have. All of us are privileged somehow. For me, it was my size. As I've gotten older, it became my stature as a prominent athlete. Today, it's my platform as a broadcaster and entertainer, which gives me privilege beyond anything my father could've imagined. When my father told me I had an obligation because of my height, I heard him. I heard him because I could see how he was of service to others. The things he had—more money than those on Skid Row, a knowledge of plumbing—were things others didn't. That gave *him* an obligation.

We help others because we have an obligation. We help others because it brings us joy. It's a simple calculation.

WE DON'T NEED A PLATFORM

In 1998, while at my brother Abdul's high school football game, my father suddenly fell out of his chair. No one knew why, but he seemed to have passed out. I got the call from my sister, Kubrat, who said that Daddy had had a stroke. I was at San Diego State at the time and drove up to see him. He appeared fine, and life went on. But more signs started appearing. My father went to my mother's friend's house to fix a plumbing issue. Sister Grace, who worked at Martin Luther King Jr. Community Hospital, noticed my father's hand trembling as he tried to write the receipt. Knowing something about the medical field, she suggested that he should get the tremor checked out, but my father, who was never one to go to a doctor, resisted. He resisted until he couldn't. The official diagnosis finally came in 2000.

When I heard the news, I was stunned—and in denial. In my eyes, my father was indestructible. His presence—physical, parental, spiritual—had dominated my life to such an extent that to imagine a world in which he was something less than powerful was almost beyond comprehension. The disease lends itself to this kind of thinking in not only its victims but the victims' loved ones. The decline is slow, a tremor here, a fainting spell there. My father looked the same, he talked the same. This nearly imperceptible progression of the disease can fool you into thinking that everything is all right. How I wanted to believe that. But then I would see his hand tremble, and the carefully constructed facade I had built to shield me from the truth would come crashing down. Naturally, my mind went to Muhammad Ali, not the man Ali was, but the man I saw during the premiere of the film dedicated to his life. The trembling shell of the mighty champ. I saw my father's future and it haunted me. And yet, what could I do, except ensure that he had the care he needed? I didn't have the money, the platform, or the know-how to do much else. My father's Parkinson's, the way I looked at it then, was just an unfortunate fact of life. We would have to live with it and try to appreciate the moments we had left with him.

I'm ashamed to admit that that was my thinking for far too long. I continued to heed the lessons my father had taught me growing up, the obligation I had to serve others. In college, I joined my first nonprofit, Athletes for Education, which sought to help inner-city kids appreciate that athletics wasn't the only way out of the hood. Education was another, more promising, avenue as well. And when I was in the NFL, I started a financial literacy campaign with Athletes for Education that took me to elementary schools to teach kids the importance of understanding how money works—a passion of mine.

My friend and former teammate Nnamdi Asomugha had started his own foundation in 2010 while still playing football. I was out of the league at the time but was inspired by Nnamdi's example. His mother, a pharmacist, had started her own foundation to help widows and orphans in need. (Nnamdi had lost his father at a young age.) Following in his mother's footsteps, Nnamdi started the Asomugha Foundation, which is focused on helping inner-city kids have access to college, another passion of mine. So when Nnamdi asked me to join the board of the foundation, I was humbled and deeply touched.

My admiration for Nnamdi was deep. I thought, here was a guy who knew exactly what he could do to help. And while I gladly accepted his invitation to join the board, I had the same worry I had when confronted with my father's Parkinson's: What could I really add? Yes, I was a former NFL player, but hardly a household name. By 2010, Nnamdi was the best cornerback in the game. Everyone knew who he was! *Of course*, he had the prestige and platform to start his own foundation. What did I have?

I stayed on the sidelines, focused on my career after football, and watching my father slowly deteriorate. I contributed where I could—all my siblings did—but there were moments when no one could be there for him. It was also in 2010 that Kabeer, who had retired from the NFL in 2008, brought my dad to live with him in Green Bay. By this point my father was on a lot of medication and he needed someone to manage all the pills he was taking, as well as assist him in his day-to-day life. My brother stepped up to the plate. Meanwhile, I didn't feel like I was contributing anything, that I wasn't doing enough for my dad. I needed a swift kick in the butt.

And then I met Jimmy Choi. Or, more accurately, I called Jimmy's run on *American Ninja Warrior* in 2017. I saw a man who had been stricken with Parkinson's at twenty-seven make it past two obstacles on the show at forty-two. Most able-bodied forty-year-olds couldn't do what Jimmy had done, and yet, before he began, I was worried that Jimmy was going to hurt himself. But what truly struck me was Jimmy's involvement with the Michael J. Fox Foundation as part of Team Fox, the fund-raising arm of the organization. Before Jimmy's run, Michael J. Fox appeared on the video screen to offer some encouraging words. And it hit me: Did Jimmy have a platform? Was he famous? Did he have the resources and financial backing to make a difference? He didn't have any of that, but still he fought.

As I recounted in chapter 2, Jimmy's daughter, who had always wanted him to try out for *ANW*, had watched a competitor with a worse condition than her father run the course. When it was over, she looked at him and asked, "What's your excuse?" That same question was now staring me in the face.

My excuse had always been: What can I do? I wasn't anyone special. I didn't have the name recognition, the prestige, the wealth to make a difference. Sure, I volunteered my time where I could with causes that interested me. And yet I could hear my younger brother, Abdul, encouraging me to do more with the platform I had. It was my obligation. Maybe my platform wasn't as big as I thought it needed to be, but it was bigger than most. Maybe I wasn't as famous as I thought I needed to be, but I had more fame than most. Maybe I wasn't as rich as I thought I needed to be, but I had enough resources.

I had more than most. A simple calculation. What's my excuse? I had none.

After the taping, I called my father. I told him to watch the episode of Jimmy's run. Then I resolved to do more. I was done with being in the back seat while I watched my father slowly but steadily deteriorate. I was done believing I had nothing to add. I ended up joining the Michael J. Fox Foundation, helping to raise awareness and funds for Parkinson's disease and research. In March 2018, I joined the board of directors.

I was on my way, but I knew I could do more. I decided to take a leap of faith and organize my own fund-raiser through the Michael J. Fox Foundation. The crew at Team Fox accepted the idea and we got to work on putting together a fund-raiser that would help people understand the critical link between exercise and how it slows the effects of the disease. The obvious choice was to hold the fund-raiser at a gym—in this case, a trampoline park in Thousand Oaks, California—with a focus on the sport parkour.

But the moment the plan was put into motion, I began to doubt myself. And this was the critical moment for me. There's a contradiction in my life, one that affects moments when I put myself out there, like the fund-raiser. I have never been comfortable with being a celebrity, for lack of a better term. To have people look up to me, admire me, respect me, just because I'm on TV goes against my natural inclination toward humility. I know that sounds odd—perhaps disingenuous—coming from someone who has chosen to make a career in front of the camera. For some, perhaps, celebrity is the goal. But my passion has never been about how people see me; it's always been about connecting with an audience. It's not about me, it's about the experience that I help facilitate.

I mention this because when I realized that I would be the draw for the fund-raiser, I suddenly felt like I couldn't do it. Who would come out to see *me*? Who cares about me beyond what I have to say on the show? And yet so much of the fund-raiser's success depended on just that—Team Fox attached my name to it for a reason. I was the celebrity. I could help drive awareness for Parkinson's research.

The other worry that gnawed at me was, even if I was a draw, would anyone care about what I cared about? It's not just an event to see me and watch some great athletes bounce around like Spider-Man. We were asking people to give their money as well. And *that's* a whole different story. Parkinson's was personal to me in perhaps the most intimate way possible. I was doing it for my father. But everyone else? What does Parkinson's mean to them? When do they think about it except when celebrities like Michael J. Fox pop up on their TVs? Or when they watch someone like Jimmy Choi amaze them? The inspiration happens for a moment, then it passes. Then they move on with their own lives and concerns.

The fears gnawed at me for months leading up to the event on August 5, 2018. My anxiety increased when the dollars weren't coming in. Perhaps I had bitten off more than I could chew? Maybe I had gotten ahead of myself on this one. Then, with a week to go, a flood. From the moment we announced the event to the event itself was about three months, although planning had been going on for nearly six months. In the final week alone, we raised roughly $35,000, bringing our total for the whole fundraiser to more than $100,000. I was overwhelmed, in tears, actually. It wasn't just my friends and friends of friends. Competitors from the show flew in from all over the country, from as far away as Alaska. Fans showed up from Indianapolis, Arizona, and elsewhere. I remember thinking, *You came out just for* this? Yes, hundreds came out for *this*. I don't think I sat for the entire four-hour event.

I learned a lot from Parkour 4 Parkinson's, but two lessons stand out. First, sometimes all you need to do is ask. People care, but they need to be asked. Everyone has busy lives and is immersed in their own problems and responsibilities. Of course, they aren't thinking about Parkinson's as much as I am. That's unrealistic. But when you ask them, when you show them how *they can help*, people respond. People want to help.

The other lesson I learned is that you don't need to have a platform to make a difference. I see the enormity of what I could accomplish *with* a platform. But how much could I have done before? How much money could I have raised when I discovered my father had Parkinson's until today? Maybe a million dollars. Maybe more. I don't know. But for years I had allowed my self-doubt to keep me from making a difference. I had a responsibility to do something productive. We all have that responsibility.

It took me many years to realize I had a duty to use my platform to find a cure for Parkinson's. It's as if I didn't want to believe this was a duty. I was struggling to make a career in broadcasting. I was struggling to raise my kids and support my family. What could I do? I could do something, and sometimes that means everything. I was overthinking my situation. I was making excuses when there weren't any. Simplify. Do what's right. Acknowledge the obligation, find the deeper meaning, and then you'll find joy in pursuing it.

SOMETHING BIGGER

It is easy to look at an obligation or a responsibility as a burden. Sometimes handling our business is a burden. We *have to* do this thing or that thing. For some, obligations can be an inconvenience. They take us away from the things we want to do. We want to sleep in, but we *have to* get up for work. It's natural that we try to minimize our responsibilities so that we have more time for ourselves. Certainly, some duties are annoyances, sometimes necessary annoyances. But these are the obligations that are part of making your way in a civilized society. We can't avoid them.

Then there are those personal responsibilities. These aren't as annoying because we can ignore them. We don't *have to* do them. We don't *have to* volunteer our time to help at a soup kitchen. We don't *have to* set aside an hour each night to help our son with his math homework. We don't *have to* give our money to a charity to help those who are less fortunate. Personal obligations are choices, and no one is going to fault us for not doing them. We can go about our lives, pursuing our dreams and providing for our families, and never acknowledge these personal obligations.

But sometimes life has a way of rubbing our faces in them, to show us just how blind we are to our own personal obligations. I had one such moment in 2011.

At the time I was taking acting lessons, which my broadcast mentor, C. S. Keys, advised that I do to feel more comfortable in front of a camera and audience, and I got an assignment to assume a character for a day. We could pick whatever character we wanted, we just had to be out in public as that character, convincing strangers of who we were. I chose to be a homeless person and I poured myself into the role. I didn't eat for a day beforehand, because I wanted to have actual hunger pangs. I didn't brush my teeth, although that didn't seem to really capture the part, so I had a bite of a brownie in the morning that turned my teeth brown. I put on some dirty clothes and did a workout, to get that sweat and funk going. I looked at myself in the mirror and saw a stinky, brown-toothed, ragged homeless man staring back at me. I was ready. I crumpled some money in my pocket and walked out the door.

My destination was the Del Amo Fashion Center, a mall in Torrance, California. I didn't have much of a plan, other than to wander around the mall and get something to eat. I tried to walk like I was weak, shuffling along, not hurrying. I must've presented quite a sight, all six feet, six inches of me, filthy, stinking. Then the magic happened. People believed I was a homeless man. I knew because I would look at the shoppers going about their day, and all of them would look away. They couldn't meet my eye. If they couldn't see me, then I didn't exist. If I didn't exist, then they wouldn't have to feel an obligation to ask if I needed something: food, water, or medicine. But when I got to the food court, the sheer mass of people meant that I would be seen as I moved among them. And I saw something I'll never forget: fear. They were afraid of me, as if I would harm them. Or offend them with my stench. I don't know what it was, but I know the feeling. It was the same fear I had when my father and I handed out donuts on Skid Row.

I continued to wander around the mall, eventually walking into a jewelry store. The woman behind the counter took one look at me and screamed—like, for real—and ran to the back of the store. My instinct was to drop the mask and tell her I was just pretending, but I stayed in character. I was having fun, and surprising myself with how well I was "acting." I wandered about the store, staring at the gold, silver, and diamonds. I didn't stay long, but I stayed long enough for someone—likely the lady behind the counter—to have called the cops. Eight officers were waiting for me outside the store, ready to handcuff me.

"What are you doing here?" one of them asked.

"Just trying to get something to eat," I mumbled. At this moment, my feelings were a mix of amusement and anger. I was amused because I knew I hadn't done anything wrong. The police were called because my presence scared someone. But scaring someone by your presence isn't a crime. But I was also angry, because I knew what was going on. I had disrupted someone else's comfort. As a homeless man who stunk and ambled, I was not supposed to be among polite society. That the cops would even hassle me reveals how deep certain biases and assumptions run in our society, even to the point that law enforcement is called in to return things to normal. I guess I expected all this at some level. I didn't dress as a homeless man and walk around Skid Row after all. I went where homeless people aren't supposed to be. I understood I was testing boundaries. Still, being confronted by eight cops would scare the pants off anyone.

But what happened next infuriated me.

"What's your name?" the cop asked.

"Akbar," I said, knowing that, despite the ruse, I probably shouldn't lie to cops.

"Do you have a last name?"

"Gbajabiamila," I replied.

The cop's eyes went wide. "From the Raiders?"

That's all it took. The cuffs were put away, the tension evaporated—at least on my end. On their end, the cops knew that they were doing something they shouldn't. I hadn't broken any law, not even the policies that governed private stores. I was wearing shoes and a shirt. But because I was homeless—someone without power or recourse—those in power felt unrestrained. My crime was disrupting someone else's comfort, and for that I was almost arrested.

I'm sure that if I just took off the mask and showed them I was "normal," then they would've let me go anyway. But I was *somebody*. Moreover, I likely had the resources to pursue a complaint against them. The tables had been turned. Now who was scared? It's crazy how that works.

Of course, they let me go, but not before an admonishment to not come back. About a year and a half later, I ran into the same cop who had questioned me outside the jewelry store. I had pulled up to the curb to pick up my son and saw a police officer nearby. I can't recall what I asked him, but we started talking. I happened to mention my little acting project, at which point the officer said, "Oh, I remember. I was there." The way he said it told me he was still a bit embarrassed. I think that was good. Perhaps my acting project helped him see the world a bit differently.

The project was extremely useful to me as well. Clearly, it opened my eyes to how we see (or don't see) others. We make value judgments based on appearances. I don't think the people who avoided me or wouldn't look me in the eye—even the one who called the cops—are bad people. They're just people who are naturally fearful of the unknown. Had I entered the mall as myself and walked up to random people asking them to donate to some homeless charity, I'm sure a lot would've given money. Some would've told me to get lost, but they would've looked me in the eye while doing so. They would've acknowledged my presence, not called the cops. But the point is that I would've walked out with more money for the homeless than when I walked in. When I walked out of the mall as a homeless person, I was almost arrested.

How people see us matters. When they see a homeless man, most people turn away. When they see someone asking them to help the homeless, many will gladly do so. Maybe we wish it wasn't this way, but we're not going to overturn human nature. People respond when those they respect call on them to do so. In 2017, when J. J. Watt of the Houston Texans tweeted a call to help raise money for victims of Hurricane Harvey, he hoped to bring in $200,000. Heck, that's impressive, even more so because I know how hard it was to raise $100,000 for Parkour 4 Parkinson's. But Watt's tweet went viral and in three weeks, he had raised $37 million. Are you kidding me?

The whole episode seems to refute my argument earlier that you don't need to have a platform to do good things. But look at it another way. There are only a handful of people in the world with a platform that could raise $37 million, and I'm not sure if I am one of them. I don't think many would have guessed that J. J. Watt, as well-known as he is in NFL circles, would have been one of them either. After all, he asked for *only* $200,000. And look what happened? Watt decided to use the platform he had to ask for help and it exploded. Even if he had raised just $200,000, that's $200,000 more than the victims of the hurricane had before Watt spent a few minutes recording himself and posting it on Twitter.

And that's the point. Watt, with a decent but hardly earth-shattering platform, spent just minutes to ask for help. It doesn't matter how much money he was able to raise; what matters is what those few minutes yielded. We don't need to make $37 million to make a difference. We don't need to have hundreds of thousands of Twitter followers to ask for help. We simply need to find a few moments out of our day to do the right thing.

I'm not speaking only of money in this case. When my father helped the homeless on Skid Row or waived a fee for his plumbing services, he felt good. Doing the right thing feels good. There's a joy to be had in helping others, a joy that we shouldn't believe is outside the role of pursuing one's dreams or striving for greatness. What, after all, are we hoping to get from achieving our dreams? Satisfaction? Yes, to be satisfied is a great reward. Fulfillment? Of course, we all want to feel fulfilled and know that our lives have meaning. But does fulfilling our dreams bring us joy?

In my experience, true joy comes only when love drives us to help our fellow man. I won't say that there aren't other sources of joy, but I will say that you aren't human if you don't get a sense of euphoria when you help someone in need. As such, it stands to reason that we should strive to help others in the pursuit of our dreams. We often think that we need to suffer to reach our dreams. That the journey must *always* be long and painful and without reward until the very end. It's true that the pursuit of dreams shouldn't be easy, but does it need to be joyless? Where is that written?

If we aren't pursuing dreams to achieve joy, then why are we pursuing them? We pursue dreams to magnify our purpose, and it is from our purpose that we are able to love more. Love is joy. The only catch in this whole design is that to experience the purest form of joy, we must help others. We must see ourselves as Jesus saw Himself: a servant of man. In short, we must tie our dreams to the service of others if we want to experience true joy in our lives. That's the calling God has for us; that's why He connected service with joy so strongly.

It took me many years to connect my career goals with this idea of service. I pursued my philanthropic efforts outside my work, volunteering my free time to help where I could. But when I saw Jimmy Choi, the connection between what I do and who I was became clear. Despite my discomfort with celebrity, I had to do something with my influence, no different than my height when I was younger. God had given me celebrity not so that I could be recognized on the street. He gave me celebrity so that I might reach others. So that I might help others.

And nothing in my career or the things I have accomplished gives me greater joy than helping find a cure for Parkinson's disease. I see the things I have pursued and achieved, and the people who have helped me along the way, as the building blocks to understand who I really am and what I really do. I once did an executive leadership course where I was asked to condense my purpose down to two words. It wasn't easy, but I was able to identify "motivate" and "assist" as the two words that most accurately and succinctly describe what my purpose is. This book is an attempt to live my purpose, to help and motivate you in leading a more successful life. I am here to fight for those who need it.

We need to fight for something bigger than ourselves if we are to realize our purpose. Because our dreams are more than our ambitions. They are God's calling to what we are here to do. No matter where our dreams reside—in whatever industry or field— they all lead to the same destination and ask the same question: Who are you fighting for?

When the greatest person I have ever known was stricken with an incurable disease, I despaired. I could see very little except for the inevitable future, a future in which he would wither before my very eyes. I saw the terrible sentence that Parkinson's had put on him, and I didn't think there was anything I could do. I certainly didn't think there would be any way to find joy in his diagnosis. I was wrong. I have found new energy unlike any I have ever experienced being part of the fight for Parkinson's patients. This energy doesn't minimize the profound grief I have for my father, but I've found that our hearts are big enough to accept both immense grief and unfathomable excitement.

I want you to feel that joy as well. Which is why I want you to attach your dreams to helping others. Fight for someone or something. Fight for an idea bigger than yourself. Fight for those who have less than you. Find your obligation and fight for it.

RELIEVE THE BURDEN

In 2006, I traveled with my father and Kabeer to Nigeria. We saw our father steadily declining in health and knew it would likely be the last time he would be able to see his birthplace before Parkinson's rendered him too frail to travel such great distances. For us brothers, it was our first visit, and for my father it was the first time he had been home since leaving in 1974. My father grew up in Lagos, on the Gulf of Guinea, which is the most populous city in Africa. The city has changed much since my father left, becoming a financial center for the entire continent, so I was amazed as we meandered through the backstreets that my father needed nothing but his memory to find the house in which he grew up. We stepped out of the car and there it was, my father's home, the one my grandfather had built. He was silent by this point, as we walked through the entryway into the courtyard. Two apple trees grew on either side of the path and my father stopped to look at them.

"Wow, look at this tree," he said, pointing to one of them. My father explained that one had been planted by his brother Nuruden, who had been killed in the civil war, and the other one—the one he was pointing at—he had planted. But the tree my father had planted had been sickly as a sapling. The family was going to uproot it, but for whatever reason didn't. Everyone assumed it would die on its own. But it didn't die. It had grown and flourished, and now its shade dominated one half of the courtyard.

"You don't know God's surprise," my father said, smiling.

We walked into the house and were standing in the living room. No one was there. My father called out.

"Alajah?"

We heard a voice from a side room.

"Who's there?"

"It's me," my father said.

"Who's me?"

"Mustapha."

"Mustapha?" A pause. "My Mustapha?"

We saw an old woman in bed, a single fan blowing against her.

The woman squinted in the darkness and saw the man standing before her. It took a moment, but a mother will always recognize her son.

"Mustapha?" she said, as if in a dream.

My father nodded, nearly overcome with emotion himself.

"Ramone! Ramone!" she suddenly screamed. An older man appeared and stared at us, at my father. He was my dad's brother.

We had come to Nigeria, and traveled to my father's childhood home, in a very different manner than when he had left at the age of twenty-seven. Then, he had $500 in his pocket and a visa, luckily earned from a chance meeting with a member of the U.S. Embassy. That was it. Thirty-two years later, my father returned, two of his children by his side.

The trip was a reminder for me about how little I knew about my father's life. I owe so much to him, not only for the lessons he taught me but also for the example he set. Yet I had never asked about where or how *he* learned these lessons. Our trip to Nigeria offered me a glimpse, but the writing of this book unearthed so many more questions. *Who* is he? Who is the man that I loved, idolized, and feared? So I sat down with him to ask him the questions that I had never asked.

The first thing he mentioned was the kindness of his own father, a Muslim imam as well as a building contractor. "People would come to him with their problems," my father explained, "and he would make sure they were happy before they left. He didn't want them to leave with any burden on their shoulders."

My grandfather, whose name was Abdul-Salaam, was a father to fourteen children, of which my dad was the seventh, right in the middle. His childhood home, the one that still stands today, is the one my grandfather built himself. He also built the mosque at which he preached. My father inherited this love for architecture and building—as well as for kindness and service.

But there were few opportunities in Nigeria, a developing country that was in the middle of the terrible Biafra War, a civil war in which six million people died. Even though the war took my father's brother, he managed to avoid military service. But one couldn't just emigrate to the United States without a highly coveted visa. By chance, my father met the American ambassador, who helped him obtain a student visa. Even then, he had to wait a year before the visa was cleared.

About his decision to leave, my father says: "There was too much corruption at home. I couldn't have a future in this country."

As for so many others, America represented hope and opportunity to my father. He never lost this conviction, even after all the terrible things that would befall us living in South Central LA. Even then, one had a future in America in a way that one didn't in Nigeria.

My father chose Los Angeles as his new home for the same reason so many others do: because of the weather. When he arrived, he didn't know a soul. He spent his first night at a halfway hotel on Santa Barbara Street (now Martin Luther King Blvd). The next day, he enrolled at the National Technical School, a trade college where he learned automotive mechanics. I asked him why automobiles and his answer is telling.

"Because," he explains, "in Nigeria my father's car had broken down and no one knew how to fix it." My father wanted to be a mechanic because he wanted to help people fix things. But his first job in America was busing tables at the airport, which he did for a year.

My father also pursued his other interest, architecture, and eventually enrolled at the Southern California Institute of Architecture. He did some work as a drafter for a company, before being let go. The world was entering the computer age, and manual drafters weren't needed anymore. Where it might take a drafter several weeks to complete designs for a building, a computer could do it in minutes. It was an important lesson for him.

"I wanted to be an entrepreneur," he says. "When you have a job, you can get fired."

What followed was a series of jobs in which my father was, more or less, in control—cabdriver, ice-cream truck driver, bus driver, and, finally, plumber. The choice of plumber was interesting, because it seemed so out of place from his other jobs. But once again, my father's explanation reveals how he looked at work. He told me that he had called a plumber to fix a problem at the house. My father watched as the plumber worked, sliding a snake down a pipe, then charging fifty dollars for it. My father thought the price was absurd.

"I knew I could do that," he says simply.

So my father flipped through the Yellow Pages and found the number for Melvin's Rooter, which was close by. He called the company and asked if they were hiring. They weren't, but they offered to take him on as an apprentice for a trial period. My father accepted, even though it meant he wouldn't be paid for a full month. After the month was over, my father made a deal with the owner to split his service charges fifty-fifty. That's how he became a plumber.

My father worked for Melvin's Rooter for about four years. When the owner wanted to decrease my father's percentage of the take, he complained. If anything, he said, he should take a higher percentage. When the owner didn't agree, my father left and formed his own plumbing business, Express Rooter.

"We had made a deal and he wanted to change it," my father says. Besides, my father knew he had enough experience to go out on his own. He purchased a used Chevrolet Van and paid to have Express Rooter in the Yellow Pages. I can still remember the random bed in the back of the van when my father bought it. He replaced it with plumbing equipment and supplies.

Other than entrepreneurship, the one strand that runs through all my father's various jobs and businesses is service. He helped his customers solve their problems, just as his own father had in his role as an imam. "Take the burden off their shoulders" is how my father explained the philosophy.

"If you see a man struggling to stand up, you help him stand," he says.

But Daddy, I pressed, didn't we need that money?

"We had enough," he says. "It's our duty to help those less fortunate than us. Those people on Skid Row, some of them were educated people. It could be you someday. One bad break and it could be you."

My parents' kindness extended to their home. We had the biggest house on the block, but it was always full, not just with the seven children, but also with strangers, usually other Nigerian immigrants who were trying to get settled in America. My parents welcomed them all in, despite the stress this would put on our financial situation. It's hard enough to feed a family of nine, but oftentimes the money would need to be stretched to feed twelve, thirteen, even fourteen people. My parents opened our home to all who needed it.

"People would come to me with a problem and I could solve it," he told me. "I can fix that. I can help."

My father had wanted to be an entrepreneur and he was for most of his life. This gave him great satisfaction, even if it didn't give him great wealth. But I know now that my father's dreams, outside his family, had little to do with ambition. They were a life of service. As a little boy, he had watched as his own father welcomed people into the home he had built and relieved the burden on their shoulders. For my father, that was a man's highest duty. Wealth, ambition, fame—what are these things except opportunities to help more people? It was the lesson he had learned from his father, and it's the greatest one I learned from him. And, boy, I learned a lot from him.

My father often would say to me that I reminded him of his own father. Now I know *why* that is perhaps the greatest gift I could've received.

10

THAT JUST HAPPENED

"**I** can't be stopped! I won't be stopped! I'm doing it for the kids!"

I screamed those words a second after I ripped off my shirt at the start of the *American Ninja Warrior* course. Yes, I was finally a competitor. After calling some four thousand runs, it was my turn. The crowd was behind me. Matt and our sideline host, Kristine Leahy, in the booth were behind me. My family—my wife, Chrystal, and our four kids—were there and behind me. My trainer and *ANW* veteran, Kevin Bull, was behind me.

What was in front of me were six obstacles. Six obstacles between me and the buzzer at the top of the Warped Wall. That was my destination. That was my goal. To everyone watching, to everyone who was behind me, they saw a confident, prepared, excited competitor about to run the gauntlet. What no one could see was that I was anything but confident. Moments before my race, I started to doubt myself again.

I can't do this. I shouldn't be here. Millions will see this! What am I thinking?

Since 2017, *ANW* has participated in Red Nose Day, which is a campaign to raise money to help end child poverty in the United States and around the world, by airing a celebrity edition of the show. The 2018 Red Nose Day special aired on May 24, although it was taped about a month earlier. Among the celebrities who participated were WWE wrestler Nikki Bella, singer-songwriter Ne-Yo, and Olympic gymnast Nastia Liukin. And me. Why me?

There are a few answers to that question. The first, most direct response is that it was my idea. I raised it during a production meeting and was met with amused looks. Me, a six-feet-six, 260-pound former NFL defensive end who hasn't even been on the climbing wall and is nearing forty? Great idea! Honestly, I think everyone thought it would make good TV—the host himself becomes the competitor. That's must-see television.

I would also be doing it for charity. For every obstacle I cleared, I would raise $5,000. That's potentially $30,000. I really had no idea how far I'd get, but the fact that it was for charity should lessen the sting of falling early. It's all for fun and it's all for the kids. The audience would love to see the host become a competitor and put his dignity on the line, and maybe they'd be inspired to give a little bit too.

The other explanation is a little more personal. As a host for five seasons, I had come to deeply respect and admire the sport and the people who had devoted their lives to it. The show's popularity has catapulted obstacle training from a niche community into one of the fastest-growing sports in the country—and the world. "Ninja gyms" have sprouted up all over America, attracting kids as young as four, as a fun, intense, and constantly changing way to get and stay fit. Many of these gyms also run their own competitions that mimic what viewers see on *ANW.*

But it's the *Ninja* community that has captured my imagination. The love that the show's veterans show to one another as well as to newcomers is truly something special. When I see the bond that forms between them I'm reminded of my old football days. Do I miss playing football? Absolutely. But I miss my teammates more; I miss what it feels like to be on a team, the way you practice together, win together, lose together, and fight together. A ninja on the show runs alone. They don't have teammates to rely on in the heat of battle. And perhaps this explains why the community is so close-knit. Because what often gets a competitor from one obstacle to the next isn't just their skills, strength, or endurance; it's the support of their fellow competitors who have traveled to be there for them. Many aren't even competing that night—or even that season. But they come out all the same. They come for their love of the sport and their love of the community, but, most important, their love for one another.

The *Ninja* community trains together. They help one another. Yes, the best ones want to win, and in that way, they are competing against one another. But they are never against one another, not in the way that two football teams are against each other on the field. Football, or really any team sport, hinges on each team wanting to crush the other one. To play at your best, you must have a little bit of animosity toward the guy facing you. That's just the way it goes. But not on *ANW.* These are some of the fiercest competitors in the world of athletics, and yet they would all gladly help their fellow ninja overcome a weakness, master an obstacle, or get to the buzzer by cheering like mad. The love they have for one another is wonderful to behold. I felt that competing would bring me closer to this wonderful community and share with them the training, the sacrifice, and the comaraderie that greets every competitor on the day of their run.

I also wanted to show my kids what it means to go after something. I wanted them to see their father set a goal and then commit to the process. Running the course was an obvious—and easily understandable—example for them. I wanted them to see the relationship between discipline and results. If I want to share in the joy of this wonderful community and raise money for children, then I need to work for it. If I didn't want to completely embarrass myself on national television, then I'd *better* work for it. We are never too old for challenges, even physical ones, and while competing on the show was never a lifelong goal of mine, I had set it as my new immediate goal. I committed. And as my father once told me twenty years earlier: "If you start something, you finish it."

THE TRAINING, AND THE PAIN

When I made the commitment to compete, I felt confident. I had about three months to train, which isn't a lot of time, but I knew I could get back into fighting shape. I sought out Kevin Bull to help me train. Kevin, who has been a regular on the show since Season 6, runs his own gym in Thousand Oaks, California, called DojoBoom. It was fifty miles from my house, but Kevin had both the resources and the skills I needed if I was serious about competing. I knew that for Kevin to even take me on as a trainee was a sacrifice for him. I also started working with a strength coach to get this old body back in shape. The lifting was natural to me, and it felt good to be back pumping all that iron for a purpose again. But training with Kevin? I was really out of my element.

My first session with Kevin lasted roughly thirty seconds. I'm not kidding. He told me to hop up on the climbing wall to warm up, and I didn't move a quarter of its length before my arms, legs, and grip went to jelly. That's when it hit me: all my strengths were weaknesses. I was built to stay on the ground, using my strength and size to push and pull, zip around corners, and fire the boosters into a dead sprint. But *Ninja* training is all up in the air, and suddenly that 260 pounds that I had learned to use to such deadly effect on the football field was just extra weight. The only thing I was pushing or pulling was myself. My speed and quickness didn't give me much of an advantage either, except perhaps for the final obstacle on the course, the Warped Wall. About the only physical trait I had that carried over to *Ninja* training was coordination— my mind and my muscles were well synchronized.

I also wasn't twenty-five anymore. Or even thirty-five. To take on *Ninja* training, I quickly learned, is to open yourself up to injuries that you thought you've outgrown. I knew I had to drop some pounds and commit to a diet high in protein to get these old muscles back to their fighting form. (I eventually dropped thirteen pounds.) I also had that bad knee, and during one attempt across a balancing obstacle I overextended it, slipping into the foam below. Man, it hurt. I limped out of the pit, knowing that my training for the day was over. The knee would heal up and I was soon back at it, but it reminded me that I might never get to the course. What if I injured myself to the point of being unable to run? It was entirely possible.

I kept at it, working with the strength coach and training with Kevin several times a week. I fit my practices in between the rest of my hectic schedule, using the relative calm of my mornings to drive the ridiculous distance to DojoBoom and back. I suppose I was getting better. After a few weeks, I could last longer than thirty seconds on the climbing wall. I had moved on to the tougher obstacles, the ones that require swinging through the air, grabbing the next ring, and then swinging again.

"Keep moving!" Kevin would say as I dangled grasping for the next ring. That's the thing with the obstacles: They require continual motion to overcome. If you stop mid-obstacle, all you're doing is letting gravity get the best of you. At my size I couldn't afford to stop; I had to keep moving. Keep moving.

Little nicks and dings would accompany the entire period of my training. The muscles just didn't recover as quickly as they used to. The body just didn't stretch and snap back the way it used to. My strength trainer, Matt Cook, was invaluable to me in this regard. I couldn't lift like I was twenty-five years old anymore. But he understood where my weaknesses were. He pushed me, but in a smart way. Because of my knees, I used to skip out on leg days. But Matt wasn't that kind of trainer. He wouldn't let me skip out on anything. The difference is that he knew how to work my leg muscles so that I not only grew stronger, but I also strengthened the muscles around my knees.

The other problem I faced was my schedule. I had never neglected my health, but there's a difference between staying fit in your late thirties and training for *ANW*. But work often kept me away from both Matt and Kevin. I couldn't focus all my energies on training. I had to burn my candle elsewhere. Work often took me away from LA, and I would have to find the time, and even another temporary trainer, to keep me on schedule. Yes, there were several moments throughout this period when I wondered what I was doing. I didn't *have to* do any of this! I could back out now and no one would know—except that my kids would know, Kevin would know, Matt would know, and I would know. They had committed to me, and I couldn't let them down.

Yet I had hit the proverbial wall in my training. Right up until the competition itself, I had never completed back-to-back obstacles. That's kind of a problem for a run that requires an athlete to complete *six* back-to-back obstacles. I had improved to the point that I felt confident completing many of the obstacles, but doing so seemed to sap all the strength and endurance from my body. Kevin saw it. "You're holding back," he said. And I was. I was fearful of injuring myself. I was exerting my body in a way that I hadn't since I was a football player, and now, on top of it, I was attempting moves that I had never done before. My holding back was all about self-preservation. A serious injury wouldn't just knock me out of Red Nose Day; it could keep me from doing my job—or being around for my wife and kids.

Would that be it? I thought. *I complete one obstacle, then I'm out?* Now, I knew that I wasn't being judged for how well I did. Just getting there at all and *trying* would be quite an achievement. But I couldn't let myself believe that completing one or two would be good enough. I knew that if I allowed myself to think this way, then I would complete only one or two. No, my goal was to complete all six. I would complete all six. Keeping that goal at the front of my mind was the only way I could make it past one.

Then, catastrophe. During my training, I felt a pop in my bicep. The pain was excruciating, and I knew this wasn't just the effects of age or a simple strain. I had done something serious. My doctor confirmed my fears when he diagnosed me with a partially torn bicep. Man, that was some tough news. The competition was only a week away.

RED NOSE DAY

Despite the injury I didn't back out. I couldn't. I had come too far, worked too hard, sacrificed too much time, and asked others to sacrifice for me only to quit now. I was entering a three-day taping schedule, with the Red Nose Day competition on the third day, which meant I was immersed in work leading up to it. The show is filmed at night, often starting around 8:00 p.m. and going until dawn. If you count the hours, these are long days. But for me they go quickly. I can lose myself in the preparation, in the runs, in the fun and excitement of the atmosphere.

Nevertheless, my own run was never far from my thoughts. Unlike all my previous days at work, as I called each run I was now comparing myself to the competitors—many of whom did quite well. *I'm really going to look like a fool.* Day two came and went and it was harder to focus on the work. My mind was in knots, and the anticipation and fear were growing with each run I called.

Then it was day three, and I was on the clock. My run was scheduled for around 1:00 a.m. I got on set that evening and felt a tightness in my chest. I was surprised and scared at how nervous I was. I kept telling myself that it was only for fun, it's for charity, and that it didn't matter how well I did. *It's for fun, it's for fun.* But I knew I was just lying to myself. I wanted to do well. I had committed myself to do well. I hadn't worked with two separate trainers, waking up at 4:00 a.m. to drive fifty miles several times a week, experienced pain and injuries, given up time with my family to fall early. Yet the burning bicep seemed to be a reminder that, no matter what others would think of my run, I was going to fail.

Moments before my run, I called Kabeer. I needed a good locker-room pep talk. He gave it to me. I don't remember being that nervous outside of my first NFL game. If anyone understood that, Kabeer would. And he knew what to say to both calm me down and focus my mind.

Then, it was my turn.

At home, viewers heard Matt say: "Get ready, because we're down to the final runner of the night and it's the one you've been waiting for." Yup, I was the last. No pressure or anything.

I did the shirt ripping, I screamed, and for those watching, they might have thought I was just doing it for the cameras. But I was really doing it to release all those nerves. Kevin was beside me. He would follow me during my run. As a celebrity competitor, the producers had decided that I could call on Kevin to do one of the obstacles for me. I didn't want to have to rely on Kevin, but with my torn bicep and knowing that each obstacle represented $5,000 for children, I couldn't let my ego get in the way. I had to accept help when I needed it.

I fly through the floating steps and lunge for the rope to swing to the next platform. Everything is going well, except I miss the landing; the rope's momentum takes me back out over the water. I steady myself and push off one of the floating steps back to the platform. Balance, balance, using those core muscles, then I stand up. I've passed the first obstacle. $5,000 for charity.

I turn to Kevin: "That's a lot harder than it looks." I wasn't saying that for the cameras either. It is harder than it looks.

The next obstacle is the Grab Bag, where you swing from a trapeze to a punching bag hanging over the water. I miss the bag on my first swing, but tackle it on the next, and my momentum carries me and the bag to the next platform. $10,000 for charity.

I let out some nerves on the platform, doing a little celebratory dance. Kevin comes close and prepares me for the next obstacle, the Spinning Bridge, which is a series of balls strung together that one must run over without disrupting too much. I begin, easily hopping over the first five balls, only to have my foot catch between the fifth and sixth ball, sending my whole body forward. As I'm falling, I think, *This is it*. But I don't feel water. I crash onto the next platform. Three obstacles completed, $15,000 raised.

Kevin must have known what I was thinking as I fell forward, because he's yelling at me on the ground, "You're safe. You're safe!"

The fourth obstacle is the Flying Shelf Grab. I don't even hesitate. I tag in Kevin to run it in my place. My bicep is burning and I know I need to reserve whatever health is left for the final obstacles. Then I watch how a master does it, using his momentum and arm strength to fly from one shelf to the next. Kevin makes it look so easy, but I know I wouldn't have made it. The obstacle requires constant strain on your arm muscles, which would've overtaxed my bicep and potentially popped it. It's also an obstacle where my size would have pulled me straight into the water. Of course, Kevin breezes through it, even doing a flip at the end to land on the platform . . . because he's Kevin Bull. $20,000.

The next obstacle is going to be the hardest. The Doorknob Drop features two boomerang-shaped boards with handholds on them that each turn on an axis. You need to pull yourself across the boomerang until it falls forward, then move across the next set of holds until you reach the second boomerang, where you do it all again before swinging yourself to the platform.

With my bicep aflame, I pull all 247 pounds of myself across the first boomerang. I extend to reach the second boomerang, grab it, and swing my other arm over, only I miss the hold. I'm hanging on to the boomerang with one arm, dangling above the water, my right arm the only thing between me and a cool dunk in the tank. With a last effort, I use my left arm—the one with the torn bicep—and reach to grab a hold and catch it. I didn't fall . . . yet. I still need to make it across this boomerang and swing to the next platform. My body is almost entirely spent; my arms feel like jelly. Somehow, I'm able to traverse the handholds, one at a time. I reach the last one, and now I need to use my momentum to jump to the platform. I start to swing, every effort sending excruciating pain through my left bicep. One swing, two swings, and I let go.

And end up on the platform. I'm on my knees, almost too tired to stand. Kevin is kneeling beside me, saying something. I find my feet and stand up. $25,000.

One more obstacle. The Warped Wall.

I see two of my children, the twins Nasir and Naomi, and I give them each a hug and kiss before turning back to the final challenge. Kevin runs up the wall first, almost teasing me with how little effort he puts into it. The crowd starts to chant, "Beat that wall! Beat that wall!" as I eye the 14.5-foot height that stands between me and the buzzer. I play a little to the crowd, holding my hand to my ear, as if to say, "Let me hear it!" Then I take off. One step, two steps, three steps, four steps, then I lunge . . . grabbing the top of the wall with my left arm, the torn bicep giving me its last ounce of strength. I pull myself up as the crowd erupts. I reach the top of the wall, do a little dance that isn't for anyone but myself, then slam my hand on the buzzer.

$30,000.

Standing atop that wall, I experience the most exhilarating moment in my athletic career. I wasn't supposed to be there. The odds were stacked against me. I was an underdog. But I made it. That just happened.

WHAT'S NEXT?

I look back on my run and I am able to reflect on how I was able to achieve something that I should not have achieved. To do something is one thing; to understand how and why you did it is something else. The power of reflection allows me to better understand where I came from and where I am going. It's like Monday-morning film study after a game. We see where we succeeded and where we failed. My kids never saw me compete in the NFL, so they never witnessed this process of striving for a tangible, definite end, or the process of reflection that is required to keep improving. My children—Elijah (seventeen), Saheedat (nine), and Nasir and Naomi (twins; six)—have watched me progress in my broadcast career, but that's just Daddy's job. What I've done and where I've succeeded in that regard will mean more to them later in life. Indeed, this book was written with them in mind, so that they understand not only what I've done, but *how* I did it.

My *Ninja* run so encapsulated the lessons I've imparted in this book that I felt ending with it would help illuminate a larger point: There comes a time in everyone's life where you will face difficulties. The "university of adversity" is one of the best experiences in life. I hope that reading about my obstacles, and how I overcame them, helps you look back on your own former (and current) difficulties and reflect on how you overcame them—or didn't. To grow in this life, we must suffer through the tough times. You will need more than motivation to succeed, because motivation is temporary. You will need the drive that can only come with a life that is fueled by purpose and tempered by trial. That drive inside you that is telling you to succeed will get you over those obstacles, those circumstances that would otherwise serve as an excuse to stay still.

The lessons in this book aren't just for those big things we want in life. They aren't just for that one lifelong dream that we have had since childhood. I wrote much of this book after my run, but when I looked back on it, I saw that what I've written here, I practiced then. I dared to believe that I could do something that I shouldn't have been able to do; I rejected the circumstances of my body, my age, my other professional and personal pursuits. I found my mentors who would help me reach my goal; I overcame the fears that gripped me in those quiet moments, between training, work, family, and life. I experienced failures when my body just wouldn't do what I asked it to do; I gave up time and sacrificed other pursuits to stay focused on my goal. I burned my candle, finding ways to train while I was on the road or just driving fifty miles to Kevin's gym, and I did it all for a cause higher than myself: I did it for charity, for the children who need that money. And I did it for my kids, so that they can see the power and joy that can come from achieving a goal you have set for yourself.

Chrystal and I come from very different backgrounds. She was raised by a single mother and I was raised by two immigrant parents. We have drawn on our unique backgrounds to provide our own children with what we hope is the best of what we learned from our parents. Yet one of the parenting goals we share is that our children will know what is required to make it in this world. They are blessed with advantages and resources neither Chrystal nor I enjoyed as kids, but these advantages can be squandered easily, just as some of the guys I grew up with squandered their talents to pursue a life in the gangs. We are all blessed with talents and advantages. And we either use them as God intended or we watch them dissipate.

My other hope is that this book provides you with the tools, lessons, and outlook to make your dreams come true. Regardless of whatever advantages you hold, or whatever circumstances in life hold you back, you can't be a passive participant. Dreams don't just happen. You might have the greatest talent in the world—or very little talent—but you need to do the actual work to turn whatever talent you have into success. I was blessed with tremendous talents. I was also saddled with unfortunate circumstances. But I learned that my talent was a gift from God and that I just had to open it up. I also learned that with perseverance, the tough times don't last.

If my story tells you something, it's that rarely is anything truly over. What I mean is that my story is littered with moments when I thought I was done, through, finished. My Achilles tendon injury should've ended my football career. (It didn't.) My NFL career should've ended after each time I was cut. (I managed to put together a four-year career.) I thought my broadcast career was finished when I took the sales job—then lost it. (I was called in to audition at the NFL Network a month later.) I thought I would be laughed out of the industry after my first season on *ANW*. (I'm now in my seventh season.) And with my aging football-player body it should have been impossible to finish the course on Red Nose Day. (I stood proudly atop that wall—with a little help from Kevin Bull.) Impossible is just an opinion, and opinions mean nothing.

Life is often long and unpredictable. Sometimes it's hard to see beyond the present moment, to look toward a day when your current failure is nothing but a lesson plan to live your life. If we had given up when faced with that failure, then none of us would be where we are. Certainly not me. But one of the greatest lessons I've learned so far is to look up, stand up, and don't ever give up. Don't let the pain push you down. Take a break when the pain, the sacrifice, or the failure becomes too much, but never give up. Remember, God has already ordered our steps, we just have to have faith. He wants us to use the gifts He has given us for His glory. The obstacles that confound your path forward are momentary. They too will pass.

We don't just encounter obstacles on the journey toward our vision. We encounter obstacles just by being alive. We encounter hardships and failures and despair even when we aren't striving for something great. In that way, the lessons in this book aren't only for your dreams; they're for how to lead a purposeful, healthier, more fulfilling life. God's calling to you might not entail a professional goal or ambition. He might just want you to be a good parent, a good spouse, a good friend, or good to yourself. We find joy in these pursuits. We find fulfillment and purpose. We don't need to worry about what's next, because what's in front of us is hard enough.

And it's that question—"What's next?"—that I am often asked. I don't like that question. It suggests that I am climbing a ladder at the top of which is some promised land. Starting at "What's next?" takes away the ability to enjoy where you are now and where you've come from. The question also leaves little room for gratitude, an appreciation of what you have. When I reached the top of the Warped Wall, I had accomplished something that to me was great. I hope that my run inspired others to do something great as well. But there's a difference between achievement and fulfillment. I wasn't going to find fulfillment at the top of that wall. My life wasn't going to suddenly fall into place, if I needed it to fall into place. I have achieved fulfillment in my life by doing the things that God calls on me to do and taking advantage of the opportunities presented along the way. "What's next?" also obscures the fact that success comes from consistency. We approach every obstacle with the same resolve and courage that we approached the last one. We don't worry about what's next; what we focus on is consistent hard work. Remember, only by consistently working hard do we achieve success. And continual success leads to greatness.

At some point, we all need to move from the passenger seat to the driver's seat. Fulfillment can come only when our life is aligned with our purpose. I am forever grateful for those who helped me, the people God put in the driver's seat before I was ready. But there comes a time when we must take over. This book is about how to take over. It's about how to use the gifts and talents God has given you to find that true joy in life. It's about how to find that purpose in your life and work relentlessly toward living it. Because we never reach our purpose; we live it. We never really get to the destination on the horizon. There isn't a promised land that will let us surrender everything, falling back into a life of leisure and ease. We are always moving forward.

Don't obsess over what comes next. The challenges will come. There will always be another obstacle. We remain present and mindful, and grateful that we aren't alone on this journey. Our dreams might look very different when compared side by side, but our paths are so very much the same. We are supposed to walk them together. We are supposed to be here. We are good enough. We can all be ninjas.

ACKNOWLEDGMENTS

Writing a book takes a lot of time, which means you need your family to be understanding and forgiving. I first want to thank my wife, Chrystal, and our kids, Elijah, Saheedat, Nasir, and Naomi, for their inspiration on this project and for their patience while I spent time away from them working on it.

I also must thank those who helped me get to the point where I can hold this book in my hands. The list begins with Kirsten Neuhaus of Foundry Literary & Media, who is more than just my literary agent. She is also the person who believed in my story and pushed me to take this great step.

I also want to thank Melinda McMullen, a longtime mentor and friend, who gave graciously of her time to help me get this book started.

And thank you to Blake D. Dvorak, with whom I collaborated to write this book. Thank you for your patience and helping me write a book that I can share with the world.

I couldn't have teamed up with a better publishing partner than Simon & Schuster. I've played on many teams, and this ranks with some of the best championship teams I've played on. I want to especially thank my editor, Cara Bedick, who helped shape this book along the way and believed in it from day one.

This book would not have been possible if I didn't have the greatest job in the world. I want to thank all the thousands of *Ninja* competitors whose runs I have had the privilege of calling the past seven years. I especially want to thank the ninjas who lent their stories to my book. It was the ninjas and their incredible stories of grit and determination that planted the seed for this book, and I thank all of them.

I also want to thank A. Smith Production and NBC for not only believing in me, but also for giving me a platform to be me, to motivate the ninjas, and to have the time of my life hosting the show. To my partner on *American Ninja Warrior*, Matt Iseman: I've learned so much about the entertainment business from you. Thank you for always being willing to share your knowledge.

We all need a push sometimes in life, and if it weren't for my manager, Alexy Posner, who pushed me to move forward with this project, I wouldn't have written a book.

Finally, I want to thank my father, Mustapha Gbajabiamila, for being an example of quiet strength as well as a huge inspiration to me throughout my life. I appreciate your contribution to my book. I can still hear your voice when I was a kid, screaming at us to "read a book!" Well, Dad, I wrote a book as well. I love you.

ABOUT THE AUTHOR

Akbar Gbajabiamila is the host of NBC's Emmy-nominated, heart-racing obstacle course competition series *American Ninja Warrior*. He also hosts Universal Kids' spin-off show *American Ninja Warrior Junior*, as well as NFL Network's highest-rated show, *NFL Fantasy Live*. He is also NBC's face of Red Nose Day 2018. He completed the Executive Certification Entrepreneurial Program from Wharton School of Business. He has appeared countless times on the *Today* show, *Rachael Ray*, *Good Morning Football*, *Entertainment Tonight*, *Access*, *Extra*, and more.